Collins

English

GCSE

Literature

work

Malcolm J. White

Malcolm Seccombe

the route to Coursework success for

AQA, Specification A

Contents

INTRODUCTION

This book has been written to help students prepare for GCSE coursework in English and English Literature (AQA Specification A). While the main objective is to develop the skills students must master to succeed in the GCSE as a whole, each of the five units specifically allows them to complete a task for their coursework folder. Opportunities for assessed Speaking and Listening tasks are also provided.

The structure of this book

There are five units in total, each covering the requirements for a particular area of coursework. These are: Shakespeare; Pre-194 Prose Study; Media; Original Writing and Post-1914 Drama. The units covering Shakespeare and pre-1914 prose are relevant to both the English and Literature GCSE, and can be used for 'cross-over' coursework.

The last section or 'Step' in each unit is called 'Tackling the Assignment' and provides possible tasks for students to use in their coursework folder. Help with planning strategies is also given. Alternative assignments based on the work covered in the unit are also provided in the Teacher's Pack.

The structure of each unit

Each unit is organised into a series of Steps that build on the practice established by the National Literacy Strategy, and lead to the writing of coursework assignments. Each step comprises:

Starting point

A starter activity, often involving the whole class and aimed at introducing themes or skills central to the Step.

Moving On

Readings and associated activities that introduce the main focus of the Step.

Development

Material which consolidates and extends the main focus of the Step, and an opportunity for students to compile notes or written pieces that will contribute to their final assignment.

Review

A chance to focus on the learning that has occurred in the Step. This work should enable students to gauge work that has been successfully covered, that which may need consolidation, and points to remember.

How to get the most from this book

A number of features appear in each unit that are designed to help students retain the knowledge they gain and apply it appropriately to their final coursework assignments. These special features are:

You Need to Know

Background information to help contextualise students' learning. These boxes often contain material about authors, literary works, as well as social and historical information.

Key Concept

A brief definition of key ideas or terms to help understand the main focus of the Step.

Assignment Watch

A summary of the main points covered in a Step to help prioritise what needs to be included for consideration in tackling assignments.

Boost Your Grade

A section at the end of each unit offers advice on Assessment Criteria, information about grades and examples of assessor comments. Exemplar coursework material is also provided which students are invited to assess for themselves.

A note from the authors to the student

You will notice that many of the activities involve you working with at least one other person, which allows for both the sharing and development of ideas. It is important that you use this opportunity to broaden your understanding of the issues.

As you work through the units, you will realise that skills learned in one unit may be applied in others. This applies particularly to your understanding of the writers' techniques, but also to aspects such as working with others, planning and organising your responses and how to improve your work.

A note from the authors to the teacher

The way in which each unit is structured enables students to:

▶ acquire knowledge, skills and understanding
▶ become familiar with assessment criteria
▶ apply their learning in a range of contexts to meet the specific requirements of GCSE
▶ structure responses
▶ improve performance through reference to model responses and commentaries.

Whilst we have chosen specific materials as the focus for the learning and the assignments themselves, you will find the model is applicable to any material of your choosing, should you wish. The texts and other materials used to exemplify the strategy and methodology in each unit were selected on the basis of our experience of what works in the classroom, the rigour with which they may be explored and their popularity with both teachers and students.

The suggested assignments may be tackled independently according to the needs of your students. However, they are structured in such a way that they could also be used cumulatively, each of them building on the one before to extend understanding and, potentially, raise achievement.

The Teachers' Pack that accompanies this book supplies schemes of work, suggested teaching notes and plans, as well as materials and ideas to support and extend students' knowledge. The worksheets included in the Teachers' Pack assist students in framing appropriate responses.

In addition to meeting the demands of the specification, we believe we have designed a course book that students will enjoy using, find both challenging and stimulating, as well as rewarding, and which will help them to develop and demonstrate their knowledge and understanding. We also believe that you will find that the materials provided in the Students' Book can be used imaginatively and flexibly.

Finally, while the skills explored within each of the units are pertinent to the specific requirements of the particular coursework assignment, the skills acquired are not discrete. Rather, they are cumulative and transferable across the units so that learning is reinforced and consolidated.

Our intention has been to provide teachers with a practical, manageable and rigorous approach to GCSE coursework. We would welcome your feedback on the books.

Malcolm J. White
Malcolm Seccombe

Shakespeare

Introduction

Objectives

In successfully completing this unit, you will:

▶ study a key scene from *Romeo and Juliet* **or** scenes relating to the supernatural from *Macbeth*

▶ understand the content, themes, characters, setting, social background, language and dramatic qualities of the scene(s) you have read

▶ take part in a variety of written and/or speaking and listening activities designed to help you to understand the text

▶ complete a written and/or oral assignment based on your chosen play.

GCSE	Coursework and Examination Skills
You will:	▶ *Reading* – analytical reading of literary texts to demonstrate understanding
▶ complete at least one GCSE speaking and listening assignment – group discussion and/or role play	▶ *Writing* – writing to present and explain complex ideas and viewpoints
▶ complete a reading assignment for GCSE English (EN2) and English Literature	▶ *Speaking and Listening* – working co-operatively with others in a group discussion
▶ develop the reading and writing skills you will need for the GCSE English Literature examination.	▶ presenting a role play.

Step 1 – *Romeo and Juliet*

In this part of the unit you are going to study Act One Scene V of *Romeo and Juliet* in detail.

Starting Point

Romeo loves Juliet from the first moment he sees her. Discuss the following questions.

1 Do you believe in the possibility of love at first sight?

2 What kind of attraction is this first love likely to be?

3 Can this kind of attraction last? Give reasons for your answers.

4 Juliet's father intends her to marry Paris. This arranged marriage would have been almost the exact opposite of Romeo and Juliet's relationship. As a class, what are your views on arranged marriage?

The ball scene from the film *Romeo + Juliet.*

Moving On

Read the following information about Act One Scene V of the play.

The scene takes place in the Capulet house in Verona, where Lord Capulet is holding a feast so that his daughter, Juliet, might meet Paris, a rich nobleman who wants to marry her. Romeo and his friends have 'gate-crashed' the party. The following extract is the scene in the play during which Romeo meets Juliet for the first time.

The scene can be subdivided into several key sections, as shown below. Read the scene in groups by sharing out the parts, and pull out the lines that refer to each section. What mood is created in each section?

Section 1: The servants prepare for the party and the guests are welcomed by Capulet.

Section 2: Capulet and his cousin talk about their youth.

Section 3: Romeo sees Juliet for the first time and is immediately captivated by her beauty.

Section 4: Tybalt recognises Romeo and sends for a weapon to kill him; he is restrained by Capulet.

Section 5: Romeo and Juliet speak and kiss for the first time.

Section 6: Romeo finds out that Juliet is a Capulet and is clearly shocked.

Section 7: As the guests leave, Juliet is distressed to discover that Romeo is a Montague.

Act One

Scene V – Capulet's house

Enter the MASKERS. SERVINGMEN *come forth with napkins*

First Servant

Where's Potpan, that he helps not to take away? He shift a trencher!   **trencher:** a plate
He scrape a trencher!

Second Servant

When good manners shall lie all in one or two men's hands,
and they unwash'd too, 'tis a foul thing.

First Servant

5   Away with the join-stools, remove the court-cubbert,   **join-stools:** stools made by a carpenter
look to the plate. Good thou, save me a piece of
marchpane; and as thou loves me let the porter let in   **court-cubbert:** sideboard
Susan Grindstone and Nell. Antony, and Potpan!   **marchpane:** marzipan

Second Servant

Ay, boy, ready.

First Servant

10   You are look'd for and call'd for, ask'd for and
sought for in the great chamber.

Third Servant

We cannot be here and there too. Cheerly, boys! Be brisk a while,
and the longer liver take all.

SERVANTS *retire*

Enter CAPULET, *with all the* GUESTS *and* GENTLEWOMEN *to the* MASKERS

Capulet

Welcome, gentlemen! Ladies that have their toes
15   Unplagu'd with corns will have a bout with you.   **have a bout:** dance
Ah ha, my mistresses! which of you all
Will now deny to dance? She that makes dainty,
She, I'll swear hath corns; am I come near you now?   **makes dainty:** hesitates to dance
Welcome, gentlemen! I have seen the day
20   That I have worn a visor and could tell
A whispering tale in a fair lady's ear,   **visor:** mask
Such as would please. 'Tis gone, 'tis gone, 'tis gone!
You are welcome, gentlemen. Come, musicians, play.
A hall, a hall! give room; and foot it, girls.   **foot it:** dance

Music plays, and they dance

25   More light, you knaves; and turn the tables up,
And quench the fire, the room is grown too hot.
Ah, sirrah, this unlook'd for sport comes well.   **unlook'd for sport:** the arrival of Romeo and friends
Nay, sit, nay, sit, good cousin Capulet,
For you and I are past our dancing days.
30   How long is't now since last yourself and I
Were in a mask?

Second Capulet
By'r Lady, thirty years.

Capulet
What, man? 'tis not so much, 'tis not so much.
'Tis since the nuptial of Lucentio,
35   Come Pentecost as quickly as it will,
Some five and twenty years; and then we mask'd.

Second Capulet
'Tis more, 'tis more: his son is elder, sir;
His son is thirty.

Capulet
Will you tell me that?
40   His son was but a ward two years ago.

Romeo [To a SERVANT]
What lady's that which doth enrich the hand
Of yonder knight?

Servant
I know not, sir.

Romeo
O, she doth teach the torches to burn bright!
45   It seems she hangs upon the cheek of night
As a a a rich jewel in an Ethiop's ear –
Beauty too rich for use, for earth too dear!
So shows a snowy dove trooping with crows
As yonder lady o'er her fellows shows.
50   The measure done, I'll watch her place of stand
And, touching hers, make blessed my rude hand.
Did my heart love till now? Forswear it, sight;
For I ne'er saw true beauty till this night.

Tybalt
This, by his voice, should be a Montague.
55   Fetch me my rapier, boy. What, dares the slave
Come hither, cover'd with an antic face,
To fleer and scorn at our solemnity?
Now, by the stock and honour of my kin,
To strike him dead I hold it not a sin.

Capulet
60   Why, how now, kinsman! Wherefore storm you so?

Tybalt
Uncle, this is a Montague, our foe;
A villain, that is hither come in spite
To scorn at our solemnity this night.

Capulet
Young Romeo, is it?

Tybalt
65   'Tis he, that villain, Romeo.

By'r lady: By our lady (the Virgin Mary)

nuptial: wedding

a ward: a minor

Ethiop: an Elizabethan word for a black African

measure: dance

forswear it: deny it

rapier: sword
antic face: comic mask
fleer: sneer

Capulet

    Content thee, gentle coz, let him alone.
    'A bears him like a portly gentleman;
    And, to say truth, Verona brags of him
    To be a virtuous and well-govern'd youth.
70   I would not for the wealth of all this town
    Here in my house do him disparagement.
    Therefore be patient, take no note of him;
    It is my will; the which if thou respect,
    Show a fair presence and put off these frowns,
75   An ill-beseeming semblance for a feast.

Tybalt

    It fits, when such a villain is a guest.
    I'll not endure him.

Capulet

    He shall be endur'd.
    What, goodman boy! I say he shall. Go to;
80   Am I the master here or you? Go to.
    You'll not endure him! God shall mend my soul!
    You'll make a mutiny among my guests!
    You will set cock-a-hoop! You'll be the man!

Tybalt

    Why, uncle, 'tis a shame.

Capulet

85   Go to, go to;
    You are a saucy boy. Is't so, indeed?
    This trick may chance to scathe you. I know what:
    You must contrary me! Marry, 'tis time –
    Well said, my hearts! – You are a princox; go.
90   Be quiet, or – More light, more light! – For shame!
    I'll make you quiet. What! – Cheerly, my hearts!

Tybalt

    Patience perforce with wilful choler meeting
    Makes my flesh tremble in their different greeting.
    I will withdraw; but this intrusion shall,
95   Now seeming sweet, convert to bitt'rest gall.

Exit

Romeo [To JULIET*]*

    If I profane with my unworthiest hand
    This holy shrine, the gentle fine is this:
    My lips, two blushing pilgrims, ready stand
    To smooth that rough touch with a tender kiss.

Juliet

100   Good pilgrim, you do wrong your hand too much,
    Which mannerly devotion shows in this;
    For saints have hands that pilgrims' hands do touch,
    And palm to palm is holy palmers' kiss.

---

portly: well-mannered

disparagement: indignity

ill-beseeming semblance: unsuitable expression

goodman boy: a yeoman (not a gentleman) and a youngster (a double insult)
mutiny: disturbance
set cock-a-hoop: cause disorder

scathe: injure
contrary: go against
princox: insolent young fellow
Cheerly, my hearts: these words are addressed to the other guests

gall: poison

holy shrine: Juliet's hand
you do wrong your hand: your hand is not so rough
mannerly: proper
palmers: pilgrims to Jerusalem who brought back palm leaves to show where they had been

Romeo
　　Have not saints lips, and holy palmers too?

Juliet
105　　Ay, pilgrim, lips that they must use in pray'r.

Romeo
　　O, then, dear saint, let lips do what hands do!
　　They pray; grant thou, lest faith turn to despair.

Juliet
　　Saints do not move, though grant for prayers' sake.

Romeo
　　Then move not while my prayer's effect I take.
110　　Thus from my lips by thine my sin is purg'd.

[Kissing her]

Juliet
　　Then have my lips the sin that they have took.

Romeo
　　Sin from my lips? O trespass sweetly urg'd!
　　Give me my sin again.

[Kissing her]

Juliet
　　You kiss by th' book.

Nurse
115　　Madam, your mother craves a word with you.

Romeo
　　What is her mother?

Nurse
　　Marry, bachelor,
　　Her mother is the lady of the house,
　　And a good lady, and a wise and virtuous.
120　　I nurs'd her daughter that you talk'd withal.
　　I tell you, he that can lay hold of her
　　Shall have the chinks.

Romeo
　　Is she a Capulet?
　　O dear account! my life is my foe's debt.

Benvolio
125　　Away, be gone; the sport is at the best.

Romeo
　　Ay, so I fear; the more is my unrest.

Capulet
　　Nay, gentlemen, prepare not to be gone;
　　We have a trifling foolish banquet towards.
　　Is it e'en so? Why, then I thank you all;
　　I thank you, honest gentlemen; good night.
130　　More torches here! [*Exeunt MASKERS*] Come on then, let's to bed.

saints: i.e. statues of saints

grant thou: i.e. grant my prayers

effect: result i.e. a kiss

by th'book: expertly, as though learned from a book

withal: with

chinks: money

dear account: terrible reckoning to pay
my life is my foe's debt: I owe my life to my enemy

towards: about to be served

Ah, sirrah, by my fay, it waxes late;
I'll to my rest.

waxes: grows

Exeunt all but JULIET *and* NURSE

Juliet
    Come hither, nurse. What is yond gentleman?
Nurse
135   The son and heir of old Tiberio.
Juliet
    What's he that now is going out of door?
Nurse
    Marry, that I think, be young Petruchio.
Juliet
    What's he that follows there, that would not dance?
Nurse
    I know not.
Juliet
140   Go ask his name. – If he be married,
    My grave is like to be my wedding bed.
Nurse
    His name is Romeo, and a Montague;
    The only son of your great enemy.
Juliet
    My only love sprung from my only hate!
145   Too early seen unknown, and known too late!
    Prodigious birth of love it is to me,
    That I must love a loathed enemy.

prodigious: ominous

Nurse
    What's this? What's this?
Juliet
    A rhyme I learnt even now
150   Of one I danc'd withal. [*One calls within* 'Juliet']
Nurse
    Anon, anon!
    Come, let's away; the strangers all are gone.

Exeunt

Development

Thinking About the Scene – Content, Characters and Themes

Talk about the following questions and keep a record of your responses.

1 How would you describe the mood of the servants at the beginning of the scene? (Lines 1–13) Explain how this helps to set the scene.

2 What do you learn about Tybalt in this scene? What does his last speech suggest about his personality, and what is likely to happen in the future?

3 Look at the lines spoken by Capulet. What kind of person is he? Give reasons for your answer.

4 Re-read the lines where Romeo and Juliet speak to each other for the first time. How do you think Juliet feels at this first meeting? Give reasons.

5 Juliet wants to find out Romeo's name. Why is she so careful about the way she questions her nurse? Think about the reason that the party is being held and Juliet's feelings for the stranger (Romeo) she has just met.

6 What are Romeo and Juliet's feelings at the end of the scene? Find evidence to support your views.

Key Concept

Whatever causes people to behave in the ways they do, is known as **motivation**.

7 What is the motivation in this scene for Romeo, Juliet, Capulet and Tybalt? Write one or two sentences on each character.

Review

What have you learned about:

▶ the structure of the scene?

▶ the characters in the scene and their motivations?

Assignment Watch

In this Step, you have examined the behaviour of the central characters in Act One Scene V. The specific examples you referred to in your answers to the questions will help you to understand *how* Shakespeare makes the audience aware of a character's motivation.

A Royal Shakespeare Company production from 1998.

Step 2 – Role Play

In this Step, you will be exploring the thoughts and feelings of characters in Act One Scene V.

Starting Point

Imagine that you work as a reporter on the society page of the *Verona Times*. You have received the photographs of the Capulet party, shown below. The report is going to appear as a photo-story, with a brief paragraph explaining the venue and purpose of the party.

1 Write the introductory paragraph, making sure you include:

▶ where and when the party took place

▶ who attended it

▶ why it was held.

2 Write captions for each of the photographs to explain what is happening in each one.

Share your work with the rest of the class.

Moving On

Choose one of the following situations and prepare a role-play presentation of three to five minutes.

A After the ball, Capulet and his wife talk about how successful they think the party has been.

B Tybalt discusses the night's events with one of his friends.

C Juliet's nurse has a conversation about the ball with one of the other servants.

Think about:

▶ the events of the party

▶ the personalities of the characters you have chosen

▶ their thoughts and feelings, and how they show them

▶ what it is that makes them behave in the ways that they do

▶ what you are trying to convey in your performance.

Tybalt recognises Romeo in the Royal Shakespeare Company production, 1998.

Development

Rehearse your performance.

Think about:

▶ the characters' gestures and movements

▶ the characters' tone of voice

▶ the parts of your characters' speeches you may want to emphasise

▶ the pacing of your performance

▶ your position on stage in relation to other characters and the audience.

Review

Perform your role play.

Remember, your teacher will ask you to explain what you were trying to convey to the audience in your presentation.

Assignment Watch

In this Step, you have thought more deeply about the characters and why they behave the way they do. You have also considered some of the techniques and devices actors need to take into account when playing a role.

Step 3 – Scene V – Shakespeare's Language

Starting Point

List eight things that you think a director has to consider when he or she is preparing a production for the stage.

Share your ideas to form a class list of a director's responsibilities.

Moving On

You are now going to examine Shakespeare's skills as a writer and dramatist.

1 Read Romeo's speech when he first sees Juliet (lines 44–53). Note that Romeo's language here is poetic.

2 Identify the figures of speech that Romeo uses and explain the impact they are intended to have on the audience. Think about the images he creates.

Key Concept

A director is the person whose job it is to prepare the staging of a play. He or she is responsible for guiding the actors and the way the play looks on stage.

two directors' interpretations of the way the scene could be staged.

Development

1 Compare Romeo's language with that of Tybalt. (Lines 53–63)

2 Look at the language Romeo and Juliet use when they speak to each other for the first time. (Lines 96–114). Note that it contains many religious references, for example, "holy shrine", "sin" and "pilgrims". Why is their conversation filled with so many religious images?

3 How do you think Juliet feels on this first meeting? Give reasons for your answer.

4 What impact does such poetic language have on the audience?

5 Shakespeare creates a range of moods or atmospheres in this scene. Discuss the changes of mood. Make a list of the changes and when they occur. What is the mood at the end of the scene?

6 Why is this scene so important to the rest of the play? Think about what has happened up to this point as well as what follows.

7 Bearing in mind the things you have considered in your study of the language in the scene, describe the effects which you, as a director, would be looking for. What would you emphasise?

Review

Share your views with rest of the class. What have you learned about:

▶ the role of a director in staging a play? Update your notes as you talk.

▶ How Shakespeare uses language to create mood and reflect character?

Step 4 – *The Dramatist and the Director*

In the first part of this Step, you will be thinking about some of the themes in Act One Scene V in order to deepen your understanding of the social context of the play. Later, you will examine the factors that contribute to good drama.

You Need To Know

In Shakespeare's day, fathers had the power to make or refuse a marriage. They would often arrange a marriage for their child with a person from a suitable family in order to confirm or increase the social standing of their own family. It was quite common for girls as young as 13 to marry much older men. A marriage contract was also financial as it included provision both for the bride's dowry and a settlement in cash and property by the husband's family, that guaranteed her welfare should the husband have died first. It was generally considered foolish to marry for love.

The best way of proving 'rank' was through liberality or generosity. People wanted to be known for their hospitality. The ideal was to have a substantial house, plenty of servants and a lavish table where anyone was welcome. A ball, such as the one held by Capulet, might be arranged to introduce the couple so that they might begin their relationship. A masked ball involved the partygoers wearing a "visor" or mask to hide their faces or identity. They might also wear fancy dress clothing.

Starting Point

1 One issue or theme that a director might like to focus on is authority. The relationship between the older and younger generations is very important throughout the play. Consider which characters are affected by this in Act One Scene V and how you might convey the importance of this onstage.

2 Which other themes or issues do you think are relevant to this scene? You may like to look at:

▸ the social structure of the period

▸ arranged marriage

▸ love at first sight (refer to the You Need to Know box to help you).

Choose two issues and find the lines from the scene that relate to it. You should be prepared to explain why they are something you would bring attention to if you were directing the play.

Share your views with the rest of the class.

Moving On

Now you are going to explore the factors that make a good drama production.

Look at the spidergram on page 18 and, with your teacher, agree what you understand by the terms shown.

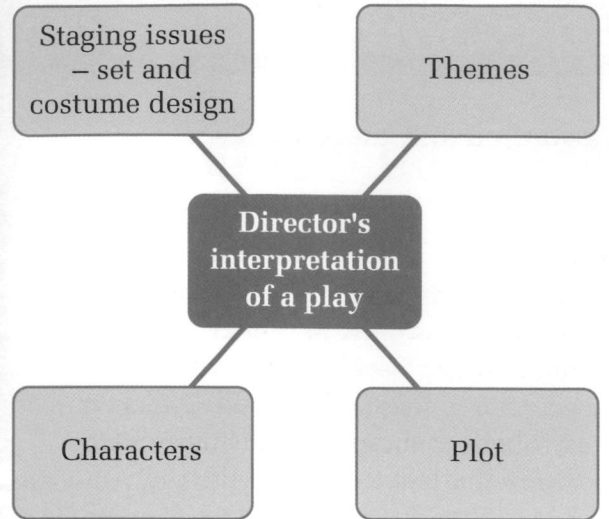

```
┌─────────────────┐        ┌─────────────┐
│  Staging issues │        │             │
│   – set and     │        │   Themes    │
│ costume design  │        │             │
└─────────────────┘        └─────────────┘
           ┌──────────────────┐
           │    Director's    │
           │  interpretation  │
           │    of a play     │
           └──────────────────┘
┌─────────────────┐        ┌─────────────┐
│                 │        │             │
│   Characters    │        │    Plot     │
│                 │        │             │
└─────────────────┘        └─────────────┘
```

Using the headings from the spidergram to help you, list the important aspects of the scene that you would wish to highlight in a production of *Romeo and Juliet*.

▶ How would you highlight these aspects on stage?

▶ What impact would you expect your direction of these aspects to have on the audience?

Make notes of why these are important features.

Share some of your thoughts with the rest of the class.

Development

Apply your understanding of the key issues in drama to answer the question: What would be the most effective way to stage Act One Scene V? You should think about:

1 the range of characters in the scene

2 the set design

3 how the costume and setting add to the impact of the scene

4 the themes that are introduced

5 the importance of this scene to the whole story

6 the possibilities it has for different interpretations, e.g. how the characters move, speak their lines, interact with each other, the kind of gestures they might make, how they might be dressed.

Review

Share your thoughts on how you would stage Act One Scene V, explaining why you would present it in the way you have chosen. Each group should take it in turns to present their interpretation of the scene.

Which of the interpretations is the most effective? Why?

Assignment Watch

In this Step, you have looked at the issues a director would consider in making a piece of drama effective. The notes you made in response to the tasks will be very useful in supporting your opinions when you tackle the assignment.

Step 5 – Tackling the Assignment

Starting Point

For your GCSE coursework folder, you will be asked to submit one of the following assignments.

Read the following questions. Choose the assignment about which you feel most confident.

Assignment 1

1 Write a set of director's notes about Act One Scene V for the actors playing *Romeo and Juliet* and production staff which gives a clear idea of:

▶ how the stage should look

▶ how the actors should be dressed

▶ how Romeo and Juliet should speak, move and behave on stage

▶ how you would emphasise the key dramatic moments

▶ why you took these decisions.

Assignment 2

2 Write a set of director's notes for each of the actors playing Romeo, Juliet, Tybalt and Lord Capulet, in which you explain and explore the characters they are playing, their relationships and the ways in which their actions during Act One Scene V affect the rest of the play.

Assignment 3

3 Why is Act One Scene V of *Romeo and Juliet* an effective piece of drama?

Moving On

Discuss with your teacher how to use the following information to help you to plan your assignment.

Planning the assignment:		
Assignment	**Thinking:**	**Structure:**
1	Think carefully about when you will set your play and how the stage set and costumes will look.	Set out the purpose of your writing.
	Consider how you will interpret the characters of Romeo and Juliet. What are their motivations? (For example, Romeo is gate-crashing a party where he might not be too welcome, while Juliet knows that the party is being thrown to introduce her to Paris.) How will this affect them?	Explain how you would interpret the play (in terms of setting and design) and why it will be interesting and appropriate for the plot.
		Explain why the scene is crucial to the rest of the play.
		Describe how you understand the motivations of the Romeo and Juliet (to the actors) – how you see them appearing on the stage, how they will react to each other and the other characters.
	Decide which are their key lines in the scene. How will you emphasize them?	Focus on the key lines they have to speak, explain why they are important and how they should be delivered (tone of voice, gestures, movements etc).
	How will they react to the other characters on stage? E.g the Nurse or Old Capulet.	Check that you have explained why you have taken these decisions.

Planning the assignment:		
Assignment	**Thinking:**	**Structure:**
2	This assignment invites you to describe, analyse and interpret characters, their relationships with each other and the dramatic contributions they make in the scene and to the play. In doing this for each character, you should think about: ▶ their personalities, feelings and motivations ▶ the relationships they have with one another ▶ how they should deliver their lines ▶ the impact of their behaviour in this scene on the rest of the play ▶ the evidence you will use to support your views.	Look again at any notes you made about this scene. In your response, make sure that you: ▶ explain the purpose of the assignment ▶ write about each character in turn – their attitudes, behaviour, relationships, and how they should speak and move ▶ explain why this scene and each of the major character's actions are important to the rest of the play ▶ support your views using evidence from the text.
3	In this assignment, you are asked to analyse, interpret and express a view about the scene. You should consider: ▶ the dramatic events of the scene ▶ Shakespeare's use of language ▶ the way the scene is structured and the changing moods suggested ▶ how Shakespeare makes use of dramatic devices such as scene shifts, the range of characters on the stage and the jumps from poetry to prose ▶ the effect that the structure and dramatic devices might have on the audience. In planning your answer you should: ▶ select key speeches and makes notes about the use of language ▶ list the points you want to make about dramatic devices and find quotes to support your ideas.	In your response, make sure that you: ▶ set out the purpose of the assignment and what you plan to write ▶ explain how Shakespeare has structured the scene, and focus on the breadth of the characters that appear ▶ analyse the different moods in the scene ▶ comment on the contrasting language in the scene giving examples of how it varies from the romantic to the aggressive (giving examples of selected quotations) ▶ discuss the effects of the shifts from poetry to prose in the scene ▶ conclude by summarising your thoughts about the scene, evaluating it's dramatic impact (how it is likely to affect an audience) and expressing a personal viewpoint.

Development

You are now going to work with others who have chosen the same assignment.

Use your preliminary notes and the bullet points in the 'Thinking' section of the Assignment breakdown to help you to develop the plan for your assignment.

Review

Discuss the notes you have made with the rest of the class. You could focus on:

- the set and costumes

- the characters' movements and gestures

- the characters – their personalities, motivations, relationships and key speeches

- Shakespeare's use of language

- the scene as a piece of drama.

(Note: Before you start to write your assignment, you should spend some time reading and assessing the 'Boost Your Grade' section on pages 48–51. In it you will find the examining board's assessment criteria, some model answers and assessor's comments. These will help you to respond successfully to your chosen assignment.)

Leonardo di Caprio and Claire Danes in the film Romeo + Juliet.

Step 1 – Macbeth – The Scottish Play

In this part of the unit, you are going to look at the play *Macbeth*. In particular, you will consider the influence of the supernatural in what happens.

First, you are going to look at the historical and social context of the play.

Below is some information, which will help you to understand how people living in the 17th century thought about witches.

Starting Point

Read the information given in the You Need to Know box about witches in the 17th century.

1 What do you think people in Shakespeare's time would have thought of witches?

2 Look up the word 'supernatural' in a dictionary. Who do you think Shakespeare's audience would credit or blame for things they couldn't understand?

3 Why do you think they might have felt this way? (Bear in mind that the Church was the most important social force at this time.)

4 What are the differences between the 17th century view of witchcraft and the modern view?

5 Why do you think these views have changed?

You Need to Know

In Shakespeare's time, people were frightened of witches because of the evil they thought they could do. Most people accused of being witches were:

- old
- poor
- female
- living alone
- not very attractive or were deformed in some way.

People believed that witches had supernatural powers, which they could use to:

- create storms
- extend the hours of darkness and shorten daylight
- create fog and mist in which to hide or cover up their evil deed (fog and mist were associated with evil because they were thought to carry disease)
- put curses on people which made them ill, or even killed them
- cause people to become possessed by the devil
- appear and disappear
- make themselves invisible
- fly.

Witchcraft was taken very seriously indeed in Shakespeare's time. If anyone was found guilty of witchcraft, they were put to death. Witches were not to be trusted – they would deliberately deceive or confuse you (sometimes just for their own amusement), and they loved to make mischief!

One of the most famous witchcraft cases was the trial of the North Berwick witches in the 1590s. The 'witches' were accused of conspiring to harm King James VI, who was travelling back from Denmark with his new bride. Their ship was caught in a violent tempest and although the royal couple survived, the storm was later blamed on a group of witches.

Having been told that she had the sign of the devil on her throat and placed under torture, a servant girl named Gelie Duncan confessed that she was one of 200 witches who under the order of the Earl of Bothwell (one of James VI's greatest enemies), gathered at the church in North Berwick. Here, the devil himself was supposed to have appeared and preached a sermon to the witches, surrounded by black candles. During this witches' coven, wax effigies of the king were burned, while a cat was baptised and thrown into the sea.

King James took these threats to his person very seriously and interrogated the witches personally. He had everyone named by Gelie Duncan brought before him. Put under great pressure, they all finally confessed and were executed.

The following law was passed by Parliament at the wish of King James in 1563, and was not repealed until 1951:

> That *"if any person shall use any invocation or conjuration of any evil or wicked spirit; Or shall consult, covenant with, entertain, employ, feed or reward any evil or cursed spirit to or for any intent or purpose; Or take up any dead man, woman or child out of the grave, – or the skin, bone, or any part of the dead person, to be employed or used in any manner of witchcraft, sorcery, charm or enchantment; Or shall use practice, or exercise any sort of witchcraft, sorcery, charm or enchantment; Whereby any person shall be destroyed, killed, wasted, consumed, pined or lamed in any part of the body; That every such person being convicted shall suffer death."*

In Scotland, between 1590 and 1680, it is estimated that 4400 witches were executed. Few cases of witchcraft were reported after 1690.

19th century engravings of the witches from *Macbeth*.

Moving On

1 Read the opening scene of the play reproduced on page 24.

2 Prepare a dramatic presentation of the scene. Think about:

▶ the setting

▶ the characters

▶ how the words would be spoken, e.g. pace, tone, volume, rhythm

▶ how the characters might move and their gestures.

Act One

Scene I – An open place.

Thunder and lightning. Enter three WITCHES

First Witch
When shall we three meet again?
In thunder, lightning, or in rain?
Second Witch
When the hurlyburly's done,
When the battle's lost and won.
Third Witch
That will be ere the set of sun.
First Witch
Where the place?
Second Witch
Upon the heath.
Third Witch
There to meet with Macbeth.
First Witch
I come Graymalkin.
Second Witch
Paddock calls.
Third Witch
Anon!
All
Fair is foul and foul is fair:
Hover through the fog and filthy air.

WITCHES *vanish*

Present your performance to the rest of the class.

The witches from the Battersea Arts Centre production, March 2000.

Development

1 Discuss the following questions. Keep a record of your responses.

a) Why do you think the scene is set on a moor in thunder and lightning?

b) Why do you think Shakespeare chose to open the play with the witches on stage?

c) What would be the audience's reaction to the witches?

d) The witches have not yet met Macbeth. What does the mention of his name suggest here?

e) What do you think they mean when they say: "Fair is foul and foul is fair"?

2 Look back at the notes on witchcraft you made at the start of the unit, and answer the following question in writing.

How does Shakespeare emphasise that the witches are evil in this first scene?

Review

What have you learned about: the way people living in the 17th century thought about witches?

How would they have reacted to the witches being present in the first scene?

Assignment Watch

In this Step, you have looked at some of the opinions a 17th century audience would have had about witches, how they might use their powers and Shakespeare's use of dramatic devices.

Step 2 – Meet Macbeth

It is assumed that by this point you will have read and/or watched the whole play, and that you are familiar with the story and the characters.

You Need to Know

Fate and Prophecy

The witches are also called the "Weird Sisters". The word 'weird' comes from the Old English word 'wryd' meaning 'fate'. The witches' prophesies are at the centre of the play. Their initial effect on Macbeth is to encourage him in his ambition.

A question often asked about Macbeth is whether the witches are able to control his behaviour, or whether he is entirely responsible for his own actions. Looking at the play, Macbeth would seem to make a deliberate choice to follow the witches' prophesies and actively set about making them come true – in other words, he consciously rejects good in favour of evil. This is in direct contrast with Banquo who instantly recognises that:

> "… oftentimes to win us to our harm,
> The instruments of Darkness tell us truths
> Win us with honest trifles, to betray's
> In deepest consequence."

Starting Point

1 Read the information in the You Need to Know box. Discuss and agree a definition for 'fate'.

2 Why do you think Shakespeare chose to call the witches the "Weird Sisters"? Think about the original meaning of the word 'weird'.

3 Use a dictionary to find modern meanings of 'weird'. What other associations does the word have?

Share your thoughts with the rest of the class.

Moving On

The first meeting between the witches and Macbeth takes place in Act One Scene III.

Read the scene reproduced on pages 26–29.

The witches from the Royal Shakespeare Company, Barbican Theatre 1993.

Act One

Scene III – A blasted heath

Thunder. Enter the three WITCHES

First Witch
Where hast thou been, sister?
Second Witch
Killing swine.
Third Witch
Sister, where thou?
First Witch
5 A sailor's wife had chestnuts in her lap,
And mounch'd, and mounch'd, and mounch'd.
'Give me,' quoth I.
'Aroint thee, witch!' the rump-fed ronyon cries.
Her husband's to Aleppo gone, master o' th' Tiger;
10 But in a sieve I'll thither sail
And, like a rat without a tail,
I'll do, I'll do, and I'll do.
Second Witch
I'll give thee a wind.
First Witch
Th'art kind.
Third Witch
And I another.
15 **First Witch**
I myself have all the other;
And the very ports they blow,
All the quarters that they know
I' th' shipman's card.
20 I will drain him dry as hay:
Sleep shall neither night nor day
Hang upon his pent-house lid;
He shall live a man forbid:
Weary sev'nights, nine times nine,
25 Shall he dwindle, peak and pine.
Though his bark cannot be lost,
Yet it shall be tempest-tost.
Look what I have.
Second Witch
Show me, show me.
First Witch
30 Here I have a pilot's thumb,
Wreck'd as homeward he did come.

Drum within

Third Witch
A drum, a drum!
Macbeth doth come.

Aroint thee: Go away
rump-fed ronyon: well-fed (probably on rump steak) worthless woman

all the other: i.e. winds
ports they blow: harbours to which the winds blow
shipman's card: i.e. compass card
pent-house lid: eyelid
forbid: cursed
bark: ship

All

The Weird Sisters, hand in hand,
35 Posters of the sea and land,
Thus do go about, about;
Thrice to thine and thrice to mine,
And thrice again, to make up nine.
Peace! The charm's wound up.

wound up: set and ready for action

Enter MACBETH and BANQUO

Macbeth

40 So foul and fair a day I have not seen.

Banquo

How far is't call'd to Forres? What are these,
So wither'd and so wild in their attire,
That look not like th' inhabitants o' th' earth,
And yet are on't? Live you, or are you ought
45 That man may question? You seem to understand me,
By each at once her choppy finger laying
Upon her skinny lips. You should be women,
And yet your beards forbid me to interpret
That you are so.

choppy: chapped

Macbeth

50 Speak, if you can. What are you?

First Witch

All hail, Macbeth! Hail to thee, Thane of Glamis!

Second Witch

All hail, Macbeth! Hail to thee, Thane of Cawdor!

Third Witch

All hail, Macbeth, that shalt be King hereafter!

Banquo

Good sir, why do you start, and seem to fear
55 Things that do sound so fair? I' th' name of truth,
Are ye fantastical, or that indeed
Which outwardly ye show? My noble partner
You greet with present grace and great prediction
Of noble having and of royal hope,
60 That he seems rapt withal. To me you speak not.
If you can look into the seeds of time
And say which grain will grow and which will not,
Speak then to me, who neither beg nor fear
Your favours nor your hate.

fantastical: imaginary

rapt withal: entranced by them

First Witch

65 Hail!

Second Witch

Hail!

Third Witch

Hail!

First Witch

    Lesser than Macbeth, and greater.

Second Witch

    Not so happy, yet much happier.

Third Witch

70   Thou shalt get kings, though thou be none.

    So, all hail, Macbeth and Banquo!

First Witch

    Banquo and Macbeth, all hail!

Macbeth

    Stay, you imperfect speakers, tell me more.

    By Sinel's death I know I am Thane of Glamis;

75   But how of Cawdor? The Thane of Cawdor lives,

    A prosperous gentleman; and to be King

    Stands not within the prospect of belief,

    No more than to be Cawdor. Say from whence

    You owe this strange intelligence, or why

80   Upon this blasted heath you stop our way

    With such prophetic greeting? Speak, I charge you.

    WITCHES *vanish*

Banquo

    The earth hath bubbles, as the water has,

    And these are of them. Whither are they vanish'd?

Macbeth

    Into the air; and what seem'd corporal melted

85   As breath into the wind. Would they had stay'd!

Banquo

    Were such things here as we do speak about?

    Or have we eaten on the insane root

    That takes the reason prisoner?

Macbeth

    Your children shall be kings.

Banquo

90   You shall be King.

Macbeth

    And Thane of Cawdor too; went it not so?

Banquo

    To th' selfsame tune and words. Who's here?

Enter ROSS *and* ANGUS

Ross

    The King hath happily received, Macbeth,

    The news of thy success; and when he reads

95   Thy personal venture in the rebels' fight,

    His wonders and his praises do contend

    Which should be thine or his. Silenc'd with that,

    In viewing o'er the rest o' th' self-same day,

    He finds thee in the stout Norweyan ranks,

imperfect: incomplete

owe: own
intelligence: information

corporal: corporeal i.e. made of flesh and blood

insane root: plant root which causes madness when eaten

100 Nothing afeard of what thyself didst make,
Strange images of death. As thick as hail
Came post with post; and every one did bear
Thy praises in his kingdom's great defence,
And pour'd them down before him.

Angus

105 We are sent
To give thee, from our royal master, thanks;
Only to herald thee into his sight,
Not pay thee.

Ross

And, for an earnest of a greater honour,

110 He bade me, from him, call thee Thane of Cawdor;
In which addition, hail, most worthy Thane!
For it is thine.

Banquo

What, can the devil speak true?

Macbeth

The Thane of Cawdor lives; why do you dress me

115 In borrow'd robes?

Angus

Who was the thane lives yet;
But under heavy judgment bears that life
Which he deserves to lose. Whether he was combin'd
With those of Norway, or did line the rebel

120 With hidden help and vantage, or that with both
He labour'd in his country's wreck, I know not;
But treasons capital, confess'd and prov'd,
Have overthrown him.

Macbeth

125 [*aside*] Glamis, and thane of Cawdor!
The greatest is behind.

[To ROSS and ANGUS]

Thanks for your pains.

[To BANQUO]

Do you not hope your children shall be kings,
When those that gave the Thane of Cawdor to me

130 Promised no less to them?

Banquo [aside to MACBETH]

That, trusted home
Might yet enkindle you unto the crown,
Besides the Thane of Cawdor. But 'tis strange;
And oftentimes to win us to our harm,

135 The instruments of darkness tell us truths,
Win us with honest trifles, to betray's
In deepest consequence.–
Cousins, a word, I pray you.

post with post: message after message

herald thee: escort you

Discuss the following questions:

1 What do you notice about the setting for this scene?

2 What are the witches doing as the scene opens?

3 The witches actually meet both Macbeth and Banquo, but they are only really interested in speaking with Macbeth. Why do you think this might be?

4 How does their conversation at this point add to the audience's impression of witches?

5 What do the witches claim will happen to Macbeth?

6 What do the witches predict for Banquo?

7 What is the significance of the news that Ross brings from the king?

Development

You are now going to consider the dramatic impact of this scene. Discuss the following questions. Keep a note of your responses.

Thinking about the witches:

1 Look at lines 1–30. How do they reinforce the audience's impression of witches?

2 In lines 33–39, the witches complete their spell against the sailor. What might this suggest to the audience about their intentions for Macbeth?

3 In what way is Banquo's description of their physical appearance appropriate for witches?

4 How do you think the audience in Shakespeare's time would have reacted to the witches?

Thinking about Macbeth:

1 What do you notice about Macbeth's first words (in line 40)? Why are they appropriate?

2 What do you think of the way Macbeth responds to what the witches say? Why? Look at what he says/thinks, and what other characters tell us about him.

3 How does this compare with the way that Banquo reacts?

4 How does Macbeth react to the news of his new title? Look at his words in lines 114–127. Note what Banquo has to say.

Share your views with the rest of the class.

Step 3 – Good and Evil – Macbeth's Soliloquy

Key Concept

When a playwright wants the audience to know what a character is thinking, he or she makes the character speak his or her thoughts out loud whilst alone on stage. This device is known as a '**soliloquy**'.

You Need to Know

The play presents a clear contrast between what is 'good' or natural and what is 'evil' or unnatural (often represented in this play by the supernatural). Macbeth has been tempted by the witches and his own ambition into killing the king and taking the throne unnaturally.

Matters such as peace of mind, a healthy appetite and deep, refreshing sleep are seen as vital to a person's well-being which is part of the natural order of things. The scene where Duncan is murdered is a decisive moment in the play, in which Macbeth chooses to repress his own nature, reject goodness and go ahead with the killing as planned.

Starting Point

1 Read Macbeth's soliloquy on page 32 and pick out two quotations from the first 10 lines that show he is in turmoil.

2 Find seven examples of words or phrases in the speech which show Macbeth's awareness of the evil involved in his plans.

Share your responses with the rest of the class.

Theo Ghil as Macbeth at the Westminster Theatre London (1999).

Roger Allen as Macbeth from a Royal Shakespeare Company production (Stratford 1996).

Act Two

Scene I, lines 33–64

Macbeth

Is this a dagger which I see before me,
The handle toward my hand? Come, let me clutch thee.
35 I have thee not, and yet I see thee still.
Art thou not, fatal vision, sensible
To feeling as to sight? or art thou but
A dagger of the mind, a false creation,
Proceeding from the heat-oppressed brain?
40 I see thee yet, in form as palpable
As this which now I draw.
Thou marshall'st me the way that I was going;
And such an instrument I was to use.
Mine eyes are made the fools o' th' other senses,
45 Or else worth all the rest. I see thee still;
And on thy blade and dudgeon gouts of blood,
Which was not so before. There's no such thing:
It is the bloody business which informs
Thus to mine eyes. Now o'er the one half-world
50 Nature seems dead, and wicked dreams abuse
The curtain'd sleep; now witchcraft celebrates
Pale Hecate's offerings; and wither'd murder,
Alarum'd by his sentinel, the wolf,
Whose howl's his watch, thus with his stealthy pace,
55 With Tarquin's ravishing strides, towards his design
Moves like a ghost. Thou sure and firm-set earth,
Hear not my steps which way they walk, for fear
Thy very stones prate of my whereabout
And take the present horror from the time,
60 Which now suits with it. Whiles I threat, he lives;
Words to the heat of deeds too cold breath gives.

A bell rings

I go, and it is done; the bell invites me.
Hear it not, Duncan, for it is a knell
That summons thee to heaven or to hell.

sensible to feeling as to sight: touchable as well as visible
heat-oppressed: feverish
marshall'st: lead

dudgeon: handle
bloody business: plans for murder
Hecate: the godess of witchcraft
alarum'd: awakened
Tarquin: infamous king of ancient Rome who raped the virtuous Lucretia
prate: talk

knell: funeral bell

Moving On

Read up to line 48 again.

1 What words does Macbeth use to describe the dagger he sees? What do these words tell you about Macbeth's feelings?

2 Macbeth tries to clutch the dagger. What does he mean when he says: "mine eyes are made fools of by the other senses"?

3 In which direction does Macbeth think the dagger is pointing?

4 Macbeth is seeing (or imagining) things. What does he 'see' happening to the dagger?

Discuss your answers with the rest of the class.

Development

Now reread lines 49–61.

1 Do you think the dagger is a supernatural sign, or does it represent Macbeth's state of mind? Give reasons for your answer.

2 Look at lines 49–51. What is Macbeth saying in these lines? What does he mean by "Nature seems dead"? Look again at the You Need to Know box on p31, as well as the box on page 34.

3 "The curtain'd sleep" is used as an image of health and restfulness, but it is being ruined by "wicked dreams". Why is this an appropriate way of describing the consequences of what Macbeth is about to do?

4 In lines 51–60, a number of supernatural images are used by Macbeth. Why are they appropriate here?

5 What does the fact that "witchcraft celebrates" at what he is about to do tell you about Macbeth's feelings about himself at this moment?

6 Murder is personified in this speech in lines 53–56. How is it described?

7 Why does Macbeth hope that the "firm-set earth" can't hear his steps?

8 What do lines 60–61 tell you about Macbeth's attitude to the murder at the end of this scene?

Using the notes you have made, answer the following question in writing. You should aim to write a minimum of 100 words.

How does this soliloquy show that he has chosen to reject goodness and embrace evil? You should comment on how the imagery he uses makes this clear.

Review

1 What have you learned about Macbeth's state of mind before he goes to murder Duncan?

2 How does this soliloquy reinforce the themes of good and evil in the play?

Assignment Watch

In this Step, you have examined the change in Macbeth's character leading up to the murder, as well as the images used to portray his state of mind.

Step 4 – Macbeth Returns to the Witches

In this Step, you are going to read the scene where Macbeth meets the witches for the second time.

You Need to Know

When thinking about the role of the natural and supernatural in *Macbeth*, it is useful to understand a concept known as the 'Divine Right of Kings', which states that the king has been chosen by God to reign. Any attempt to remove a king from power is therefore an act against the natural order of things and against God. King James I (Shakespeare's patron at the time of writing *Macbeth*) believed very strongly in the Divine Right of Kings. He wrote in Chapter 20 of his *Works*:

The state of monarchy is the supremest[1] thing upon earth; for kings are not only God's Lieutenants[2] upon earth, and sit upon God's throne, but even by God himself are called gods...I conclude then this point touching the power of kings with this axiom[3] of divinity[4]. That as to dispute what God may do is blasphemy...[5]

Footnotes

[1] supremest: the most important
[2] Lieutenants: junior officers; used here to mean God's representatives on Earth
[3] axiom: a statement or saying that is generally accepted to be true
[4] divinity: religious belief
[5] blasphemy: showing disrespect to God

Starting Point

Having read the information in the You Need to Know box, consider the following questions:

1 What do you think the 17th century view of regicide (killing the king) would have been?

2 Why is it appropriate that Macbeth's murder of Duncan is started by a supernatural, unholy source – the witches?

Share your thoughts with the rest of the class.

Moving On

Now read the scene reproduced on pages 35–40. You will see that by this stage, Macbeth has seized the throne having murdered Duncan. He has also murdered Banquo. It is the appearance of Banquo's ghost at the banquet that causes him to seek out the witches again. His personality has changed considerably. You will be examining how the witches behave towards Macbeth and his reactions to what they tell him.

The Third Apparition from Act IV Scene 1. Roger Allam as Macbeth in the Royal Shakespeare Company production, 1996.

Act Four

Scene I – A dark cave. In the middle, a cauldron boiling

Thunder. Enter the three WITCHES

First Witch
5   Thrice the brindled cat hath mew'd.
Second Witch
    Thrice and once the hedge-pig whin'd.
Third Witch
    Harpier cries; 'tis time, 'tis time.
First Witch
    Round about the cauldron go;
    In the poison'd entrails throw.
10   Toad, that under cold stone
    Days and nights has thirty-one
    Swelter'd venom sleeping got
    Boil thou first i' th' charmed pot.
All
    Double, double toil and trouble;
15   Fire burn, and cauldron bubble.
Second Witch
    Fillet of a fenny snake,
    In the cauldron boil and bake;
    Eye of newt, and toe of frog,
    Wool of bat, and tongue of dog,
20   Adder's fork, and blind-worm's sting,
    Lizard's leg, and howlet's wing –
    For a charm of pow'rful trouble,
    Like a hell-broth boil and bubble.
All
    Double, double toil and trouble;
25   Fire burn, and cauldron bubble.
Third Witch
    Scale of dragon, tooth of wolf,
    Witch's mummy, maw and gulf
    Of the ravin'd salt-sea shark,
    Root of hemlock digg'd i' th' dark,
30   Liver of blaspheming Jew,
    Gall of goat, and slips of yew
    Silver'd in the moon's eclipse,
    Nose of Turk, and Tartar's lips,
    Finger of birth-strangled babe
35   Ditch-deliver'd by a drab –
    Make the gruel thick and slab;
    Add thereto a tiger's chaudron,
    For th' ingredients of our cauldron.

brindled: streaked
hedge-pig: hedgehog
Harpier: the Third witch's familiar

swelter'd: sweated

fenny: marsh
howlet's: owl's

maw and gulf: throat and stomach
ravin'd: stuffed
slips of yew: cuttings of a yew tree (which are poisonous)
Ditch-delivered by a drab: born to a prostitute in a ditch
slab: slimy and sticky
chaudron: guts

All
>Double, double toil and trouble;
40 > Fire burn, and cauldron bubble.

Second Witch
>Cool it with a baboon's blood,
>Then the charm is firm and good.

Enter HECATE

Hecate
>O well done! I commend your pains;
>And every one shall share i' th' gains.
45 > And now about the cauldron sing,
>Live elves and fairies in a ring,
>Enchanting all that you put in.

[Music and a song: 'Black spirits, etc.' Exit HECATE*]*

Second Witch
>By the pricking of my thumbs,
>Something wicked this way comes. *[Knocking]*
50 > Open, locks, whoever knocks.

Enter MACBETH

Macbeth
>How now, you secret, black, and midnight hags!
>What is't you do?

All
>A deed without a name.

Macbeth
>I conjure you by that which you profess –
55 > Howe'er you come to know it – answer me.
>Though you untie the winds and let them fight
>Against the churches; though the yesty waves
>Confound and swallow navigation up;
>Though bladed corn be lodg'd and trees blown
60 > down;
>Though castles topple on their warders' heads;
>Though palaces and pyramids do slope
>Their heads to their foundations; though the treasure
>Of nature's germens tumble all together,
65 > Even till destruction sicken – answer me
>To what I ask you.

First Witch
>Speak.

Second Witch
>Demand.

Third Witch
>We'll answer.

a deed without a name: too horrible to be described

that which you profess: i.e. witchcraft

yesty: frothing like fermenting yeast

swallow navigation: sink ships
germens: the very seeds of life

First Witch

70   Say, if thou'dst rather hear it from our mouths,
        Or from our masters?

Macbeth

        Call 'em; let me see 'em.

First Witch

        Pour in sow's blood, that hath eaten
        Her nine farrow; grease that's sweaten

75   From the murderer's gibbet throw
        Into the flame.

All

        Come, high or low;
        Thyself and office deftly show!

Thunder. FIRST APPARITION, *an Armed Head*

Macbeth

        Tell me, thou unknown power –

First Witch

80   He knows thy thought.
        Hear his speech, but say thou nought.

Apparition

        Macbeth! Macbeth! Macbeth! Beware Macduff;
        Beware the Thane of Fife. Dismiss me. Enough.

He descends

Macbeth

        Whate'er thou art, for thy good caution, thanks;

85   Thou hast harp'd my fear aright. But one word more –

First Witch

        He will not be commanded. Here's another,
        More potent than the first.

Thunder. SECOND APPARITION, *a Bloody Child*

Apparition

        Macbeth! Macbeth! Macbeth!

Macbeth

        Had I three ears, I'd hear thee.

Apparition

90   Be bloody, bold, and resolute; laugh to scorn
        The pow'r of man, for none of woman born
        Shall harm Macbeth. *[Descends]*

Macbeth

        Then live, Macduff; what need I fear of thee?
        But yet I'll make assurance double sure

95   And take a bond of fate. Thou shalt not live;
        That I may tell pale-hearted fear it lies,
        And sleep in spite of thunder.

our masters: the devils who the witches serve
farrow: piglets
sweaten: sweated, oozed out
gibbet: gallows

harp'd: guessed

take a bond of fate: hold fate to its word

Thunder. THIRD APPARITION: *a Child Crowned, with a tree in his hand*

What is this
That rises like the issue of a king,
100   And wears upon his baby brow the round
And top of sovereignty?

All

Listen, but speak not to't.

Apparition

Be lion-mettled, proud, and take no care
Who chafes, who frets, or where conspirers are:
105   Macbeth shall never vanquish'd be until
Great Birnam wood to high Dunsinane Hill
Shall come against him. *[Descends]*

Macbeth

That will never be.
Who can impress the forest, bid the tree
110   Unfix his earth-bound root? Sweet bodements, good!
Rebellion's head, rise never till the wood
Of Birnam rise, and our high-placed Macbeth
Shall live the lease of nature, pay his breath
To time and mortal custom. Yet my heart
115   Throbs to know one thing; tell me, if your art
Can tell so much – shall Banquo's issue ever
Reign in this kingdom?

All

Seek to know no more.

Macbeth

I will be satisfied. Deny me this,
120   And an eternal curse fall on you! Let me know.
Why sinks that cauldron? And what noise is this?

Hautboys

First Witch

Show!

Second Witch

Show!

Third Witch

Show!

All

125   Show his eyes, and grieve his heart;
Come like shadows, so depart!

A Show of Eight Kings, and BANQUO *last; the last king with a glass in his hand*

Macbeth

Thou art too like the spirit of Banquo; down!
Thy crown does sear mine eye-balls. And thy hair,

issue: child
round and top of sovereignty: a crown
who chafes, who frets: who rages and storms

impress: conscript (i.e. make the trees march)
bodements: prophecies
lease of nature: the full term of human life

Hautboys: a high pitched wooden instrument

sear: burn

130   Thou other gold-bound brow, is like the first.
    A third is like the former. Filthy hags!
    Why do you show me this? A fourth? Start, eyes.
    What, will the line stretch out to th' crack of doom?
    Another yet? A seventh? I'll see no more.
135   And yet the eighth appears, who bears a glass
    Which shows me many more; and some I see
    That two-fold balls and treble scepters carry.
    Horrible sight! Now I see 'tis true;
    For the blood-bolter'd Banquo smiles upon me,
140   And points at them for his. *[The show vanishes]*
    What! is this so?

First Witch
    Ay, sir, all this is so. But why
    Stands Macbeth thus amazedly?
    Come, sisters, cheer we up his sprites,
145   And show the best of our delights;
    I'll charm the air to give a sound,
    While you perform your antic round;
    That this great king may kindly say,
    Our duties did his welcome pay.

Music. The WITCHES *dance, and vanish*

Macbeth
150   Where are they? Gone? Let this pernicious hour
    Stand aye accursed in the calendar.
    Come in, without there.

Enter LENNOX

Lennox
    What's your Grace's will?
Macbeth
    Saw you the Weird Sisters?
Lennox
155   No, my lord.
Macbeth
    Came they not by you?
Lennox
    No, indeed, my lord.
Macbeth
    Infected be the air whereon they ride;
    And damn'd all those that trust them! I did hear
160   The galloping of horse. Who was't came by?
Lennox
    'Tis two or three, my lord, that bring you word
    Macduff is fled to England.

Start, eyes: Macbeth would rather not have eyes than see this
crack of doom: doomsday (the end of the world)
blood-bolter'd: covered in blood

antic round: grotesque dance

Macbeth

    Fled to England!

Lennox

    Ay, my good lord.

Macbeth [aside]

165   Time, thou anticipat'st my dread exploits.
    The flighty purpose never is o'ertook
    Unless the deed go with it. From this moment
    The very firstlings of my heart shall be
    The firstlings of my hand. And even now,
170   To crown my thoughts with acts, be it thought and done:
    The castle of Macduff I will surprise,
    Seize upon Fife; give to the edge o' th' sword
    His wife, his babes, and all unfortunate souls
    That trace him in his line. No boasting like a fool:
175   This deed I'll do before this purpose cool.
    But no more sights! – Where are these gentlemen?
    Come, bring me where they are.

Exeunt

flighty purpose: intentions
never is o'ertook: is never carried out

the very … my hand: Macbeth plans to act on emotion without thought

Rufus Sewell as Macbeth with the three witches – Queens Theatre, London 1999.

Discuss the following questions on Act Four Scene I.

1 The witches are making a powerful potion before Macbeth arrives. How do the ingredients reinforce the sense of evil?

2 What are the prophesies of the apparitions?

3 How does Macbeth interpret them?

Share your responses with the rest of the class.

Development

You are now going to look at how Macbeth has changed from the beginning of the play up to this point.

(Note: Your teacher may choose to use this activity as an assessment for GCSE speaking and listening.)

1 Build up a portrait of the kind of person Macbeth was at the start of the play. For example, was he loyal to his king? Was he a loving husband? You may wish to look at the Sergeants' lines in Act One Scene II (lines 8–23), as well as Duncan's words to him in Act One Scene IV (lines 14–21).

2 Discuss the following questions. Keep a record of your responses and remember to refer to specific examples to support what you say.

How does Macbeth feel and behave when he hears what each apparition says?

How would you describe Macbeth's frame of mind/mood at the end of this scene? Think about what he has heard from the apparitions. Think about his attitude towards Macduff in particular.

How does Macbeth's frame of mind influence his behaviour from this point?

How does Macbeth's attitude change when he finally realises that he has been deceived by the witches and that his children will not be king?

3 Now you are going to consider the way the witches are represented in this scene. How does this scene reinforce the audience's impression of the witches?

Look at where the scene is set; refer to the stage directions; think about what they say; consider how they treat Macbeth (remember he is the king).

Write about 100 words to explain the effect of the witches' words on Macbeth from this scene to the end of the play. You may wish to look at Act Four Scene II, Act Five Scene III, Act Five Scene V (the last 20 lines), Act Five Scene VII and Act Five Scene VIII (lines 8–34).

Review

1 What have you learned about the 17th century view of the authority of kings?

2 Can you explain how and why Macbeth has changed since the beginning of the play?

3 What kind of king is Macbeth?

Assignment Watch

In this Step, you have examined some of the things that have influenced Macbeth's behaviour and mental condition since the beginning of the play. It is important that you have a clear understanding of what causes Macbeth to change.

Step 5 – King and Country

In this Step, you will examine the ways in which Scotland suffers after Macbeth becomes king.

Starting Point

Any organisation needs a set of rules to ensure that it runs smoothly and provides stability. Schools, for example, will have a Code of Conduct to provide an orderly atmosphere for staff and pupils. These sets of rules outline the rights and responsibilities of all members of the organisation. Without them, there is likely to be chaos.

Some rules are created to ensure good order around the workplace or school, e.g. 'Don't run in the corridor'. Other rules are designed to promote principles such as fairness, e.g. 'No bullying'.

1 Look at a copy of your own School Rules. Choose three and identify the reasons (or principles) why they have been created.

2 Now think about the play, *Macbeth*. Name three of the principles a good king should use to provide good order for his country.

Share your findings with the rest of the class to agree a set of principles for good government of a country.

Moving On

The following extract from Act Three Scene VI shows how Lennox and another Lord feel about the way Macbeth is ruling Scotland. They talk about some of the recent events and Macbeth's part in them.

Read the extract below and on page 43 and answer the questions on page 44.

Act Three

Scene VI – Forres. The palace

Enter LENNOX *and another* LORD

Lennox
My former speeches have but hit your thoughts,
Which can interpret farther. Only I say
Things have been strangely borne. The gracious Duncan
Was pitied of Macbeth. Marry, he was dead.   5
And the right-valiant Banquo walk'd too late;
Whom, you may say, if't please you, Fleance kill'd,
For Fleance fled. Men must not walk too late.
Who cannot want the thought how monstrous
It was for Malcolm and for Donalbain   10
To kill their gracious father? Damned fact!

> **My … thoughts:** my recent words have only coincided with what you have in your mind
> **borne:** managed
> **who cannot want the thought:** who can fail to think

How it did grieve Macbeth! Did he not straight,
In pious rage, the two delinquents tear,
That were the slaves of drink and thralls of sleep?
15 Was not that nobly done? Ay, and wisely too;
For 'twould have anger'd any heart alive
To hear the men deny't. So that, I say,
He has borne all things well; and I do think
That had he Duncan's sons under his key –
20 As, an't please heaven, he shall not – they should find
What 'twere to kill a father; so should Fleance.
But peace! For from broad words, and 'cause he fail'd
His presence at the tyrant's feast, I hear,
Macduff lives in disgrace. Sir, can you tell
25 Where he bestows himself?

Lord

The son of Duncan,
From whom this tyrant holds the due of birth,
Lives in the English court, and is receiv'd
Of the most pious Edward with such grace
30 That the malevolence of fortune nothing
Takes from his high respect; thither Macduff
Is gone to pray the holy King upon his aid
To wake Northumberland and warlike Siward,
That by the help of these – with Him above
35 To ratify the work – we may again
Give to our tables meat, sleep to our nights,
Free from our feasts and banquets bloody knives,
Do faithful homage and receive free honours –
All which we pine for now. And this report
40 Hath so exasperate the King that he
Prepares for some attempt of war.

Lennox

Sent he to Macduff?

Lord

He did; and with an absolute 'Sir, not I!'
The cloudy messenger turns me his back
45 And hums, as who should say, 'You'll rue the time
That clogs me with this answer.'

Lennox

And that well might
Advise him to a caution, t' hold what distance
His wisdom can provide. Some holy angel
50 Fly to the court of England and unfold
His message ere he come, that a swift blessing
May soon return to this our suffering country
Under a hand accurs'd!

Lord

I'll send my prayers with him.

Exeunt

thralls: slaves
under his key: locked up
for from broad words: because of frank talk

the holy king: Edward
upon his aid: on Malcolm's behalf
with Him above to ratify the work: with God to strengthen their activities

1 List the crimes Macbeth is accused of committing.

2 List the words used to describe Macbeth, Duncan, Banquo, and Edward – the English king. How do they differ?

3 What do these words suggest about the noblemen's attitude to Macbeth and the way he is running the country?

4 Re-read the last 29 lines. What do they suggest is missing in Scotland under Macbeth's rule?

Share your responses with the rest of the class.

Development

You are now going to look at four short extracts that refer to Scotland under Macbeth's rule.

Read the extracts and answer the questions on page 45.

Extract 1
Macduff
Let us rather
Hold fast the mortal sword, and like good men
Bestride our down-fall'n birthdom. Each new morn
New widows howl, new orphans cry; new sorrows
Strike heaven on the face, that it resounds
As if it felt with Scotland and yell'd out
Like syllable of dolour.
(Act Four Scene III, lines 2–8)

dolour: pain

Extract 2
Macduff
Bleed, bleed, poor country.
Great tyranny, lay thou thy basis sure,
For goodness dare not check thee. Wear thou thy wrongs,
The title is affeer'd. Fare thee well, lord.
I would not be the villain that thou think'st
For the whole space that's in the tyrant's grasp
And the rich East to boot.
(Act Four Scene III, lines 31–37)

Extract 3
Macbeth
Bring me no more reports; let them fly all.
Till Birnam wood remove to Dunsinane
I cannot taint with fear. What's the boy Malcolm?
Was he not born of woman? The spirits that know
All mortal consequences have pronounc'd me thus:
'Fear not, Macbeth; no man that's born of woman
Shall e'er have power upon thee'. Then fly, false thanes,
And mingle with the English epicures.
The mind I sway by and the heart I bear
Shall never sag with doubt nor shake with fear.
(Act Five Scene III, lines 1–10)

Extract 4

Macduff

O, I could play the woman with mine eyes
And braggart with my tongue! But, gentle heavens,
Cut short all intermission; front to front
Bring thou this fiend of Scotland and myself;
Within my sword's length set him; if he scape,
Heaven forgive him too!

Malcolm

This tune goes manly.
Come, go we to the King. Our power is ready;
Our lack is nothing but our leave. Macbeth
Is ripe for shaking, and the pow'rs above
Put on their instruments. Receive what cheer you may;
The night is long that never finds the day.

(Act Four Scene III, lines 230–240)

1 What do these extracts add to your understanding of:

a) how people have come to view Macbeth?

b) the state of Scotland?

Note evidence from the extracts to support what you say in each case.

2 What is Macbeth's frame of mind in Act Five?

Share your views with the rest of the class.

<table>
<tr><td>

Review

1 What have you learned about what makes a good king?

2 How has Scotland suffered under Macbeth's rule?

</td><td>

Assignment Watch

As you know, Macbeth is an unnatural king who has usurped the throne through murder, spurred on by the prophesies of the evil supernatural witches. In this Step, you have looked at the effects that his reign has on Scotland – important when considering the role of the supernatural in the play.

</td></tr>
</table>

Step 6 – Tackling the Assignment

Starting Point

For your GCSE coursework folder, you will be asked to submit one of the following assignments.

Read the following questions. Choose the assignment about which you feel most confident.

Assignment 1

1 What significance does Act One Scene I have for the play as a whole?

Assignment 2

2 How does Shakespeare use the witches to influence the audience's reactions?

Assignment 3

3 What is the role of the supernatural in the play?

Moving On

Read the section below that relates to your chosen assignment. Use it to help you to make a preliminary plan for your assignment.

Planning the assignment:		
Assignment	**Thinking:**	**Structure:**
1	For this question you should: ▶ bear in mind the impression created by the witches' appearance in the opening scene ▶ think about how they set the tone for what follows in the play ▶ consider the words the witches use, the stage directions, the settings. ▶ note the audience's knowledge of witchcraft and the supernatural.	Look again at any notes you made about this scene. In your response, make sure that you: ▶ explain the aims and purpose of your writing ▶ describe briefly what happens in this scene ▶ comment on how the audience would react and what they would understand by the presence of the witches ▶ explain the relevance of this scene for the rest of the play ▶ express a personal opinion about the scene.
2	For this question, you need to: ▶ consider the witches influence on Macbeth's thoughts and actions ▶ show understanding of the audience's knowledge of the supernatural. ▶ find examples of the language used by the witches that is intended to provoke a reaction from the audience. (Note: You may wish to draw evidence from other parts of the play, especially Act One Scene VII, Act Two Scenes I and II, and Act Three Scene IV.)	In your response, make sure that you: ▶ explain the aims and purpose of your writing ▶ explore the effect the witches have on events ▶ examine the ways in which Shakespeare uses the witches to make an impact on the audience ▶ summarise your views and express an opinion about how effectively these things are done.

Planning the assignment:		
Assignment	**Thinking:**	**Structure:**
3	This is a more open-ended question. You need to consider the following: ▶ the way the witches are presented to the audience ▶ the way Shakespeare's audience would have reacted to the supernatural ▶ the powers the witches have and how much influence they have over Macbeth ▶ the amount of responsibility the supernatural must take for what happens to the other characters ▶ the role of the 'natural order' of things and the Divine Right of Kings in the play ▶ the effect that Macbeth's unnatural, tyrannical reign has on Scotland. (Note: You may wish to draw evidence from other parts of the play, especially Act One Scene VII, Act Two, Scenes I and II, Act Three Scene IV, Act Four Scene III and Act Five, Scene VII)	Set out the aims and purpose of your writing. Explain how the audience in Shakespeare's lifetime would have reacted to the supernatural. Explain how much power the witches have over Macbeth at the beginning of the play and as it progresses. Convey how Shakespeare presents the contrast between a natural, holy king (Edward) and the unnatural tyrant Macbeth. Make clear how much you think the supernatural is to be blamed for what happens in the play.

Development

You are now going to work with others who have chosen the same assignment.

Use your preliminary notes and the bullet points in the 'Thinking' section of the assignment breakdown to help you to develop the plan for your assignment.

Review

Discuss the notes you have made with the rest of the class. Think about:

▶ the impact the appearance of the witches has on the audience in Act One Scene I

▶ how the audience is made aware of the nature of witchcraft and the influence it can have

▶ how Macbeth's reaction to the witches changes during the play

▶ the different ways in which modern audiences and those in Shakespeare's time might react to the powers of the supernatural.

(Note: Before you start to write your assignment, you should spend some time reading the 'Boost Your Grade' section on pages 48–51 that the examining board will use to assess your response and discuss them.)

Boost Your Grade

Here is a set of criteria against which you can measure your answer. The criteria apply to EN2 (Reading) and/or Literature assessment.

Starting Point

Read the criteria and make a note of anything that you do not understand.

Discuss any concerns you may have about the criteria.

Criteria

Grade E	You should:
	▷ show familiarity with the play's events and characters
	▷ describe its themes and ideas
	▷ show familiarity with Shakespeare's language
	▷ mention the play's social, historical and cultural context
	▷ describe the play's impact on the audience
	▷ refer to aspects of the test when explaining your views.
Grade C	You should show insight when discussing:
	▷ the events, characters, structure and stagecraft of the play
	▷ the issues raised in the play, their implications and relevance to Shakespearean and modern audiences
	▷ Shakespeare's use of language.
Grade A	You should show analytical and interpretative skills when evaluating:
	▷ the moral issues raised in the play
	▷ how Shakespeare uses dramatic devices to explore the play's themes and ideas. Shakespeare's use of language and imagery to achieve specific dramatic and poetic effects
	▷ how Shakespeare exploits the social, historical and cultural context of the play.

Moving On

1 Read the following excerpts taken from a student's response to Assignment 2 for *Macbeth*, and the assessor's comments which follow.

2 Find evidence from the excerpt to support what the assessor says about the work.

◖Excerpt 1◗

This excerpt was written in response to Assignment 2 for Macbeth.

The audience would know what to expect when the witches begin the play. They would expect them to interfere with Macbeth and know that were just out to trick or confuse him. Shakespeare was aware of this understanding and he used it right at the start of the play by having the witches in Scene I. By doing this, Shakespeare is letting the audience know that witches and the supernatural are going to influence events in the play. Even though it is a very short scene, he immediately links Macbeth's name with the witches when they say that their next meeting will be:

Upon the heath

there to meet with Macbeth

He also hints at the trouble they are going to cause when they say:

Fair is foul and foul is fair

which suggests that bad things will be seen as good and good things seen as bad.

Assessor's Comments

This student clearly understands the **historical setting** of the play and the way that Shakespeare's audience would respond to the witches. He or she also begins to comment on **Shakespeare's use of language** and what it suggests about the events of the play. The comments, however, are restricted to Shakespeare's language. The opportunity to **comment on stagecraft**, the witches' appearance and their movements and gestures is not shown here. However if this extract is representative of a full response, this candidate is touching the criteria for a grade C.

Share your thoughts with the rest of the class.

> Another device used effectively is that of contrast. The way in which Shakespeare weaves elements such as love and hate, and the calm of Capulet's experience against the hot-headed nature of Tybalt's youth is clearly designed to start the audience thinking about their potential impact for the "star-crossed lovers". The poetry we hear in the words from Romeo's own lips suggest how smitten he is by Juliet's beauty. The simile in which he compares her to "a rich jewel in a Ethiop's ear" and the metaphor of "a snowy dove trooping with crows" reflects his romantic nature. Tybalt's lines contrast sharply. He is openly vindictive in his attitude towards Romeo, using words like "foe", "villain" and "spite" to show his contempt for him. His view that Romeo has come "to scorn at our solemnity this night" is starkly different to the sensitivity already displayed by Romeo. It is obvious from this point that Tybalt's anger is not going to make Romeo and Juliet's relationship an easy one. This juxtaposition of love and hate heighten the sense of drama and anxiety.
>
> It is only the intervention of Capulet at this point that brings some calm to the situation.

Assessor's Comments

Having dealt with the **social, historical and cultural context** of the play earlier, this student moves on to demonstrate her/his analytical, interpretative and evaluative skills. S/he deals with the way Shakespeare **uses contrast to heighten tension** and to establish the characters of Romeo and Tybalt. There is clear evidence of the student **using selective quotation effectively** to support her/his comments. There is also **analysis of the style of language** used by both of the characters in this part of the scene. Overall, therefore, this is a sophisticated and well written piece that was awarded a grade A.

◖Development◗

Read the following two excerpts taken from assignments in response to *Macbeth* and *Romeo and Juliet*. One was awarded Grade E and the other a Grade A.

Use the assessment criteria to write assessor's comments for each excerpt. Give examples to support each comment.

Excerpt 3

This excerpt was written in response to Assignment 1 for Romeo and Juliet.

The actor playing the part of Juliet should stand out from the crowd at the party. She should be dressed in white so that she looks beautiful and like an angel. She should look like a 'swan'. As soon as she sees Romeo she should look like she is impressed by him, love at first sight. The audience will know that the party is meant to introduce Juliet to Paris and that Juliet is attracted to the wrong person. She will show how much she is in love by asking the Nurse for Romeo's name. She should not do this openly because she is not going along with her father's hopes. When she learns that he is a Montague, she should look shocked because he is a sworn enemy of her family.

Excerpt 4

This excerpt was written in response to Assignment 3 for Macbeth.

It is clear that Shakespeare wanted his audience to be aware of the impact of the forces of darkness on the events of the play. He wanted to show that once someone is tempted, they can come to depend on evil and reject goodness. In Macbeth, we have a character who appears to have everything going for him. He is considered a good, loyal subject who has fought bravely to defend his king and country from invasion and betrayal. Consequently, he is thought of very highly by everyone around him, including the king. They describe him in glowing terms as "Bellona's bridegroom" or "worthy gentleman". He is going to be richly rewarded for his efforts.

In addition, he has a close, loving relationship with his wife. So what is it that turns him into a "hellhound" and a "butcher"; a man who can plot the murder of his best friend Banquo and the innocent wife and children of Macduff? Whilst Macbeth himself admits he is driven by ambition:

I have no spur to prick the sides of my intent

save vaulting ambition

it is the witches who set it free to cause havoc and destruction. It is the witches who lure him with false promises when they first meet and trap him with apparent invincibility in Act Four Scene I.

Review

What have you learned about writing a successful GCSE Shakespeare assignment?

Prose Study

Introduction

Objectives

In successfully completing this unit, you will:

▶ Analyse in detail three extracts from *Great Expectations* by Charles Dickens or *The Strange Case of Dr Jekyll and Mr Hyde* by Robert Louis Stevenson.

▶ develop understanding of:
  – plot
  – characters
  – themes/issues
  – how writers organise or structure writing
  – how writers' use of language creates characters with whom we sympathise
  – how writers manipulate the readers' reactions to characters

▶ develop the ways in which you respond to literary texts

▶ identify the key features of writing about literary texts

▶ plan your response to an assignment question

▶ draft/revise/proofread your response

▶ present your final piece of work for GCSE assessment.

GREAT EXPECTATIONS
BY CHARLES DICKENS

DR JEKYLL & MR HYDE

GCSE
You will:
▶ complete a GCSE Reading/Literature coursework assignment
▶ develop the reading skills you need for the GCSE examination
▶ complete a GCSE Speaking and Listening component in both group discussion and formal presentation.

Coursework and Examination Skills
▶ *Reading* – analytical reading of fiction
▶ *Writing* – writing to show understanding, analysis and evaluation of a major author's work (literary criticism)
▶ *Speaking and Listening* – working co-operatively with others in a group discussion; working with others in a group presentation.

Step 1 – Great Expectations

Starting Point

From the beginning, it is important that you understand that all writers make *careful* choices from a range of techniques and devices that shape their writing to engage and interest their readers. You might like to think of this as the storytellers' set of skills and devices, or 'tool kit'.

Before you begin you will need to become familiar with the techniques writers use in their work to affect the way the readers feel.

The terms and definitions below have been jumbled up. Match each definition with its appropriate term by writing the corresponding letter and number, e.g. '2–k'.

Share and agree your answers with another student.

Discuss your answers with the rest of the class.

1 Setting	**a** The place(s) and time in which the story takes place.
2 Characterisation	**b** The atmosphere created by the author, e.g. gloomy, tense or romantic.
3 Structure	**c** The final paragraph(s) which brings the story/chapter to a satisfactory conclusion.
4 Opening	**d** The sequence in which the author presents the incidents in the story.
5 Ending	**e** The words spoken by the characters that inform the reader of their personality, motivation and attitudes, or which are used by the author to develop or explain events in the story.
6 Dialogue	**f** The introductory paragraph(s), which may set the scene, mood or tone of the piece, or which might introduce important character(s).
7 Mood	**g** The choice made by the author to write either as an observer (in the third person) or as a participant (in the first person) in the story.
8 Voice	**h** The range of sentence types used by the author to engage and sustain the readers' interest and to reinforce aspects like attitude, tone, mood, etc.
9 Vocabulary	**i** The author's choice of words that create vivid settings, events and characters, and that establish mood.
10 Punctuation	**j** The use of sentence markers to clarify meaning.
11 Sentence variety	**k** The development of the personality, motivation and attitudes of the people involved.

Moving On

Now that you have discussed some of the ways in which writers work, you are going to apply your understanding to analyse the first of three extracts taken from *Great Expectations* by Charles Dickens.

You Need to Know

Dickens and *Great Expectations*

Charles Dickens was born on 7 February, 1812. When his father (a naval clerk who continually spent more money than he made) was imprisoned for debt in 1824 in Southwark, the 12-year-old Charles was removed from school and sent to work in a blacking factory to help support his family. Dickens considered this to be the most terrible time in his life.

This childhood poverty and adversity contributed greatly to Dickens' later views on social reform in a country in the throes of the Industrial Revolution, and to his compassion for the lower classes – especially the children. The inscription on his tombstone in Westminster Abbey reads: "He was a sympathiser to the poor and the suffering and the oppressed; and by his death, one of England's greatest writers is lost to the world".

Society, class and money are all themes that occur again and again in Dickens' fiction. Perhaps as a result of his childhood experience of poverty, many of his novels deal with the problems characters have making their way in the world from difficult starts. *Oliver Twist, David Copperfield, Nicholas Nickleby* and *Great Expectations* all follow this pattern. It is worth bearing in mind that in Dickens' time, not having money could have truly disastrous consequences – the poor house or debtors' prison being just two of the possibilities.

Charles Dickens.

Great Expectations is the story of Philip Pirrip, known as Pip, an orphan raised by his sister and her husband, Joe Gargery. It follows the ups and downs of his life from when he is a young, poor boy living near the Thames estuary to when he moves to London, where he hopes to become a successful 'gentleman'.

This is one of Dickens' most well known and popular novels, both at the time it was written and with modern-day readers. He is thought of as a 'people watcher', observing closely the extremes in the social conditions and lifestyles of the wealthy middle classes and the grinding poverty of the working classes. In telling the story, Dickens draws on his knowledge and experiences of real-life personalities to create vivid characters.

The story takes place in early nineteenth-century England and begins in a semi-rural setting. We first meet Pip as a very young, impressionable boy, and in this first chapter from the novel, he is visiting the graves of his parents and brothers and sisters.

The extract on pages 55–57 describes Pip's first meeting with an escaped convict, Abel Magwitch, who becomes an important influence on his life.

Read the following extract.

Great Expectations

Extract 1 – Pip and Magwitch

My father's family name being Pirrip, and my Christian name Philip, my infant tongue could make of both names nothing longer or more explicit than Pip. So, I called myself Pip, and came to be called Pip.

I give Pirrip as my father's family name, on the authority of his tombstone and
5   my sister – Mrs Joe Gargery, who married the blacksmith. As I never saw my father or my mother, and never saw any likeness of either of them (for their days were long before the days of photographs), my first fancies regarding what they were like, were unreasonably derived from their tombstones. The shape of the letters on my father's, gave me an odd idea that he was a square, stout, dark man,
10 with curly black hair. From the character and turn of the inscription, *'Also Georgiana Wife of the Above,'* I drew a childish conclusion that my mother was freckled and sickly. To five little stone lozenges, each about a foot and a half long, which were arranged in a neat row beside their grave, and were sacred to the memory of five little brothers of mine – who gave up trying to get a living
15 exceedingly early in that universal struggle – I am indebted for a belief I religiously entertained that they had all been born on their backs with their hands in their trouser-pockets, and had never taken them out in this state of existence.

Ours was the marsh country, down by the river, within, as the river wound, twenty miles of the sea. My first most vivid and broad impression of the identity of
20 things, seems to me to have been gained on a memorable raw afternoon towards evening. At such a time I found out for certain, that this bleak place overgrown with nettles was the churchyard; and that Philip Pirrip, late of this parish, and also Georgiana wife of the above, were dead and buried; and that Alexander, Bartholomew, Abraham, Tobias and Roger, infant children of the aforesaid, were
25 also dead and buried; and that the dark flat wilderness beyond the churchyard, intersected with dykes and mounds and gates, with scattered cattle feeding on it, was the marshes; and that the low leaden line beyond was the river; and that the distant savage lair from which the wind was rushing, was the sea; and that the small bundle of shivers growing afraid of it all and beginning to cry, was Pip.

30 "Hold your noise!" cried a terrible voice, as a man started up from among the graves at the side of the church porch. "Keep still, you little devil, or I'll cut your throat!"

A fearful man, all in coarse grey, with a great iron on his leg. A man with no hat, and with broken shoes, and with an old rag tied round his head. A man who had
35 been soaked in water, and smothered in mud, and lamed by stones, and cut by flints, and stung by nettles, and torn by briars; who limped, and shivered, and glared and growled; and whose teeth chattered in his head as he seized me by the chin.

"Oh! Don't cut my throat, sir," I pleaded in terror. "Pray don't do it, sir."

"Tell us your name!" said the man. "Quick!"

40 "Pip, sir."

"Once more," said the man, staring at me. "Give it mouth!"

"Pip. Pip, sir."

"Show us where you live," said the man. "Point out the place."

I pointed to where our village lay, on the flat inshore among the alder-trees

45 and pollards, a mile or more from the church.

The man, after looking at me for a moment, turned me upside-down, and emptied my pockets. There was nothing in them but a piece of bread. When the church came to itself – for he was so sudden and strong that he made it go head over heels before me, and I saw the steeple under my feet – when the church came to itself, I say, I was
50 seated on a high tombstone, trembling, while he ate the bread ravenously.

"You young dog," said the man, licking his lips, "what fat cheeks you ha' got."

I believe they were fat, though I was at that time undersized for my years, and not strong.

"Darn me if I couldn't eat 'em," said the man, with a threatening shake of his
55 head, "and if I han't half a mind to't!"

I earnestly expressed my hope that he wouldn't, and held tighter to the tombstone on which he had put me; partly to keep myself upon it; partly to keep myself from crying.

"Now then, lookee here!" said the man. "Where's your mother?"
60 "There, sir!" said I.

He started, made a short run, and stopped and looked over his shoulder.

"There, sir!" I timidly explained. "'Also Georgiana.' That's my mother."

"Oh!" said he, coming back. "And is that your father alonger your mother?"

"Yes, sir," said I; "him too; late of this parish."
65 "Ha!" he muttered then, considering. "Who d'ye live with – supposin' you're kindly let to live, which I han't made up my mind about?"

"My sister, sir – Mrs Joe Gargery – wife of Joe Gargery, the blacksmith, sir."

"Blacksmith, eh?" said he. And looked down at his leg.

After darkly looking at his leg and at me several times, he came closer to my
70 tombstone, took me by both arms, tilted me back as far as he could hold me; so that his eyes looked most powerfully down into mine, and mine looked most helplessly up into his.

"Now lookee here," he said, "the question being whether you're to be let to live. You know what a file is?"
75 "Yes, sir."

"And you know what wittles is?"

"Yes, sir."

After each question he tilted me over a little more, so as to give me a greater sense of helplessness and danger.
80 "You get me a file." He tilted me again. "And you get me wittles." He tilted me again. "You bring 'em both to me." He tilted me again. "Or I'll have your heart and liver out." He tilted me again.

I was dreadfully frightened, and so giddy that I clung to him with both hands, and said, "If you would kindly please to let me keep upright, sir, perhaps I
85 shouldn't be sick, and perhaps I could attend more."

He gave me a most tremendous dip and roll, so that the church jumped over its own weather-cock. Then, he held me by the arms, in an upright position on the top of the stone, and went on in these fearful terms –

"You bring me, tomorrow morning early, that file and them wittles. You bring
90 the lot to me, at that old Battery over yonder. You do it, and you never dare to say a word or dare to make a sign concerning your having seen such a person as me,

or any person sumever, and you shall be let to live. You fail, or you go from my
words in any partickler, no matter how small it is, and your heart and your liver
shall be tore out, roasted and ate. Now, I ain't alone, as you may think I am.
95 There's a young man hid with me, in comparison with which young man I am a
Angel. That young man hears the words I speak. That young man has a secret way
pecoolier to himself, of getting at a boy, and at his heart, and at his liver. It is in
wain for a boy to attempt to hide himself from that young man. A boy may lock
his door, may be warm in bed, may tuck himself up, may draw the clothes over
100 his head, may think himself comfortable and safe, but that young man will softly
creep and creep his way to him and tear him open. I am a-keeping that young
man from harming of you at the present moment, with great difficulty. I find it
wery hard to hold that young man off your inside. Now, what do you say?"

I said that I would get him the file, and I would get him what broken bits of
105 food I could, and I would come to him at the Battery, early in the morning.

"Say, Lord strike you dead if you don't!" said the man.

I said so, and he took me down.

"Now," he pursued, "you remember what you've undertook, and you
remember that young man, and you get home!"
110 "Goo-good-night, sir," I faltered.

"Much of that!" said he, glancing about him over the cold wet flat. "I wish I
was a frog. Or a eel."

At the same time, he hugged his shuddering body in both his arms – clasping
himself, as if to hold himself together – and limped towards the low church wall.
115 As I saw him go, picking his way among the nettles, and among the brambles
that bound the green mounds, he looked in my young eyes as if he were eluding
the hands of the dead people, stretching up cautiously out of their graves, to get
a twist upon his ankle and pull him in.

When he came to the low church wall, he got over it like a man whose legs
120 were numbed and stiff, and then turned round to look for me. When I saw him
turning, I set my face towards home, and made the best use of my legs. But
presently I looked over my shoulder, and saw him going on again towards the
river, still hugging himself in both arms, and picking his way with his sore feet
among the great stones dropped into the marshes here and there, for stepping-
125 places when the rains were heavy, or the tide was in.

The marshes were just a long, black, horizontal line then, as I stopped to look
after him; and the river was just another horizontal line, not nearly so broad nor
yet so black; and the sky was just a row of long, angry, red lines and dense black
lines intermixed. On the edge of the river I could faintly make out the only two
130 black things in all the prospect that seemed to be standing upright; one of these
was the beacon by which the sailors steered – like an unhooped cask upon a pole
– an ugly thing when you were near it; the other a gibbet, with some chains
hanging to it which had once held a pirate. The man was limping on towards this
latter, as if he were the pirate come to life, and come down, and going back to
135 hook himself up again. It gave me a terrible turn when I thought so; and as I
saw the cattle lifting their heads to gaze after him, I wondered whether they
thought so too. I looked all round for the horrible young man, and could see no
signs of him. But, now I was frightened again, and ran home without stopping.

Pip and Magwitch from a 1974 adaptation of the novel.

The Purpose of the Opening

Dickens chooses to begin the novel in this way in order to establish an understanding of Pip's background, the setting for the first part of the story and, most importantly, to establish the readers' sympathy for Pip, the central character.

Key Concept

The term **'voice'** refers to the choice made by the author to write either as an observer (third person) or as a participant in the story (first person).

If the writer chooses to use **the third person**, the characters will be referred to with words like 'he', 'she', 'they' and 'them'. The writer tells the story as an observer might, describing what is happening in front of him or her.

If the writer selects **the first person**, the story is told by one of the participants. The author uses words like 'I', 'me', 'mine' or 'my'.

In groups, discuss your responses to the questions opposite and be ready to feed back

your answers to the class. Remember to find evidence to support what you say.

1 What information are you given about Pip's background?

2 What information are you given about where he is?

3 How are we supposed to feel about him?

4 Are you given any information about Magwitch's background?

5 How is he presented to the reader?

6 How are you supposed to feel about him?

7 What 'voice' does Dickens use in this extract?

8 If a novel is narrated in the first person by one of the characters in the story, is there anything you need to bear in mind?

9 Do you think the story would be the same if told by another character from the novel?

10 Are there any advantages or disadvantages to telling a story in this way?

Discuss your thoughts with your teacher.

Development

Key Concept

In presenting their ideas, writers choose to organise them in a particular order or way. This aspect of their work is known as the **structure**.

1 Look back at the first two paragraphs of the extract and decide how the skills listed in the writers' tool kit have been used by Dickens. Make sure you think about the following: structure, voice, setting, tone and vocabulary, and be prepared to comment on each one.

2 Now, you will look at another section from the extract and report back on how it contributes to the purpose of the novel's opening to the rest of the class. Your teacher will allocate you a section of the text.

▶ Take the section you have been given to look at. Read through it to form an initial impression of its content.

▶ Think about things that happen in the section, including the order in which they happen and how they are described.

▶ Remember to make sure that you are able to comment on the voice, tone and vocabulary used.

▶ Discuss your thoughts with the other members of your group.

3 Present your findings to the rest of the class, and look together at the way in which Dickens has structured the opening to the novel. How has he achieved his purpose of setting the scene and introducing the main character to the reader?

An illustration from the 1885 edition.

Review

1 What do you understand by the term 'writers' tool kit'?

2 What have you learned about the time in which Dickens was writing?

3 What have you learned about Pip and Magwitch?

4 What have you learned about the structure of this first extract?

Assignment Watch

In this Step you have been looking at the way in which Dickens structures the opening to *Great Expectations* and the techniques he has used to do so. The understanding you have gained of how he achieves this will help you to tackle the coursework assignments for this unit.

Step 2 – Creating Character and Mood: Pip and Magwitch

Starting Point

1 Read the following outline.

Tom has arranged to meet Sacha and Rashid at an old house on the outskirts of town. The house has been empty for a long time.

You will be given a mood word from the following list:

> sad   frightening   humorous
> tense   threatening

2 In pairs, write a short descriptive piece based on the outline suggested above. Make sure that you include details to suggest the mood you have been given. Think carefully about the words you use and how you will achieve your desired effect. You should write 50 to 100 words. Think about:

▶ why they are going there

▶ where the house is

▶ who might have lived in the house

▶ what the house looks like

▶ why the house may now be empty.

One of you will read out your piece of writing. At the end of the reading, the rest of the class will try to identify the mood you and your partner were trying to create.

Key Concept

Mood and character are created by the careful selection of particular vocabulary and phrases.

Moving On

You are going to examine the way Dickens applies this skill in the first extract.

1 Find at least ten examples of words, phrases or sentences in the extract that describe Magwitch, the setting and what he says. Set them in a table as follows. Some have been done for you.

Magwitch	Setting	What he says
A fearful man	A bleak place overgrown with nettles	"your liver shall be tore out, roasted and ate".

Do not copy out whole or large parts of sentences, but be selective!

2 Select five of your examples and say what impression of the setting or Magwitch these words create. Set them in a table as follows:

Words	Impressions
fearful bleak	These words help to emphasize the cold, frightenening atmosphere

Dickens decided to write *Great Expectations* to be serialised in the weekly journal he edited, mainly because its sales were falling – another author's novel was going down badly with the public.

As he was starting the novel, Dickens wrote the following, giving us an insight into what he intended to achieve:

"The book will be written in the first person throughout, and, and during these first three weekly numbers, you will find the hero to be a boy-child like David (Copperfield). Then he will be an apprentice. You will not have to complain of the want of humour as in *The Tale of Two Cities*. I have made the opening, I hope, in its effect exceedingly droll. I have put a child and a good-natured foolish man, in relations that seem to me very funny."

Robert De Niro as Magwitch in the 1997 film adaptation.

Development

Some might see Magwitch as simply a villain who is terrifying a small boy. Others might view him in a more sympathetic light. Using the information you have gathered, decide which view you agree with and write a short piece to explain why you feel this way. Bear in mind:

▶ the way he speaks. Does he speak in a distinctive way? Is there any phonetic spelling? What effect does this have?

▶ what he says. Do you think he would hurt Pip? Look closely at the extract when considering your reply.

Review

1 What have you learned about the word 'mood', as used by writers, and about how a writer creates mood and character?

2 What have you learned about Magwitch's character? What about the setting?

Assignment Watch

In this Step, you have been focusing on the choice of vocabulary Dickens makes in creating 'character' and 'mood'. These are two devices from the tool kit that Dickens uses to affect the way we think and feel about the story and its characters. The examples you have collected will prove invaluable when you write your assignment.

You have also looked at the social backgrounds of Pip and Magwitch. The defenceless, terrified orphan boy and the desperate, freezing, starving convict both engage the reader's sympathy in different ways.

Step 3 – Revealing Character – Miss Havisham

You are now going to study another extract from *Great Expectations* and analyse how Dickens influences the reader's feelings about the characters he describes.

Background to the extract

In the extract on p.63, Pip visits Miss Havisham, a wealthy lady whom he has never met before and who lives a very strange life with only her ward, Estella, for company. Miss Havisham has taken legal responsibility for the upbringing of Estella, even though they are not related. Although Pip's invitation to the house is considered a great honour for him, he is nevertheless, anxious about meeting the old lady and keen on not disgracing himself or his family.

Starting Point

Social class and appearance are things that matter a great deal in the novel. Pip becomes aware of his dress and education in the next extract you will consider.

Are people still concerned with these things today? If so, which things matter in particular?

As a class, compile a list of things that are important if someone is to have a high social standing where you live.

Victorian gentlemen.

You Need to Know

In the extract that follows, Pip understands (for the first time) that there are people who will look down on him as a 'common labouring-boy', if he remains a blacksmith's apprentice.

Many people received no schooling at all at this time. As someone who was being educated, Estella's reaction to him would have been the same as many others of the middle and upper classes. The 'working classes' were perceived as the lowest rungs of society, representing uncleanliness (disease was viewed with horror as medicine was still primitive), as well as the threat of social unrest if they should come together to form a 'mob'.

Furthermore, it was easy to slip down the rungs of society. There was no welfare state and so if you had no money, your options were often to turn to crime, to beg on the streets, to go to the poorhouse or to end up in a debtors' prison.

The time that Dickens spent working in a blacking factory, while his parents were in a desperate financial position, informed his view of what it was like to occupy a lowly status in society – and fired his determination to make something of himself. It is possible that there are echoes of Dickens' own experiences in the character of Pip when later in the novel, he becomes embarrassed to be working with Joe in the forge:

"I used to stand about the churchyard on Sunday evenings when night was falling, comparing my perspective with the windy marsh view, and making out some likeness between them by thinking how flat and low they both were…"

Moving On

Now read the extract below.

Extract 2 – Miss Havisham

I entered, therefore, and found myself in a pretty large room, well lighted with wax candles. No glimpse of daylight was to be seen in it. It was a dressing-room ... and prominent in it was a draped table with a gilded looking-glass ... In an arm-chair, with an elbow resting on the table and her head leaning on that hand,
5   sat the strangest lady I have ever seen, or shall ever see.

She was dressed in rich materials – satins, and lace, and silks – all of white. Her shoes were white. And she had a long white veil dependent from her hair, and she had bridal flowers in her hair, but her hair was white. Some bright jewels sparkled on her neck and on her hands, and some other jewels lay sparkling on
10 the table. Dresses, less splendid than the dress she wore, and half-packed trunks, were scattered about. She had not quite finished dressing, for she had but one shoe on – the other was on the table near her hand – her veil was but half arranged, her watch and chain were not put on, and some lace for her bosom lay with those trinkets, and with her handkerchief, and gloves, and some flowers, and
15 a Prayer-Book, all confusedly heaped about the looking-glass.

It was not in the first moments that I saw all these things, though I saw more of them in the first moments than might be supposed. But I saw that everything within my view which ought to be white, had been white long ago, and had lost its lustre, and was faded and yellow. I saw that the bride within the bridal dress
20 had withered like the dress, and like the flowers, and had no brightness left but the brightness of her sunken eyes. I saw that the dress had been put upon the rounded figure of a young woman, and that the figure upon which it now hung loose, had shrunk to skin and bone ...

"Who is it?" said the lady at the table.
25 "Pip, ma'am."

"Pip?"

"Mr Pumblechook's boy, ma'am. Come – to play."

"Come nearer; let me look at you. Come close."

It was when I stood before her, avoiding her eyes, that I took note of the
30 surrounding objects in detail, and saw that her watch had stopped at twenty minutes to nine, and that a clock in the room had stopped at twenty minutes to nine.

"Look at me," said Miss Havisham. "You are not afraid of a woman who has never seen the sun since you were born?"

I regret to state that I was not afraid of telling the enormous lie
35 comprehended in the answer, "No."

"Do you know what I touch here?" she said, laying her hands, one upon the other, on her left side.

"Yes, ma'am."

"What do I touch?"
40 "Your heart."

"Broken!"

She uttered the word with an eager look, and with strong emphasis, and with a weird smile that had a kind of boast in it ...

"I am tired," said Miss Havisham. "I want diversion, and I have done with
45 men and women. Play ...

"I sometimes have sick fancies," she went on, "and I have a sick fancy that I want to see some play. There, there!" with an impatient movement of the fingers of her right hand; "play, play, play!"

50 ...I felt myself so unequal to the performance that I stood looking at Miss Havisham in what I suppose she took for a dogged manner, inasmuch as she said, when we had taken a good look at each other –

"Are you sullen and obstinate?"

"No, ma'am, I am very sorry for you, and very sorry I can't play just now...It's so new here, and so strange, and so fine – and melancholy – " I stopped, fearing I
55 might say too much, or had already said it, and we took another look at each other.

Before she spoke again, she turned her eyes from me, and looked at the dress she wore, and at the dressing-table, and finally at herself in the looking-glass.

"So new to him," she muttered, "so old to me; so strange to him, so familiar to me; so melancholy to both of us! Call Estella."

60 As she was still looking at the reflection of herself, I thought she was still talking to herself, and kept quiet.

"Call Estella," she repeated, flashing a look at me. "You can do that. Call Estella. At the door."

... [When the girl appeared] Miss Havisham beckoned her to come close, and
65 took up a jewel from the table, and tried its effect upon her fair young bosom and against her pretty brown hair. "Your own, one day, my dear, and you will use it well. Let me see you play cards with this boy."

"With this boy! Why, he is a common labouring-boy!"

I thought I overheard Miss Havisham answer – only it seemed so unlikely –
70 "Well! You can break his heart."

"What do you play, boy?" asked Estella of myself with the greatest disdain.

"Nothing but beggar my neighbour, miss."

"Beggar him," said Miss Havisham to Estella. So we sat down to cards.

It was then I began to understand that everything in the room had stopped, like
75 the watch and the clock, a long time ago. I noticed that Miss Havisham put down a jewel exactly on the spot from which she had taken it up. As Estella dealt the cards, I glanced at the dressing-table again, and saw that the shoe upon it, once white, now yellow, had never been worn. I glanced down at the foot from which the shoe was absent, and saw that the silk stocking on it, once white, now yellow,
80 had been trodden ragged. Without this arrest of everything, this standing still of all the pale decayed objects, not even the withered bridal dress on the collapsed form could have looked so like grave-clothes, or the long veil so like a shroud.

So she sat, corpse-like, as we played at cards; the frillings and trimmings on her bridal dress looking like earthy paper. I knew nothing then of the discoveries
85 that are occasionally made of bodies buried in ancient times, which fall to powder in the moment of being distinctly seen; but I have often thought since, that she must have looked as if the admission of the natural light of day would have struck her to dust.

"He calls the knaves, Jacks, this boy!" said Estella with disdain, before our first
90 game was out. "And what coarse hands he has. And what thick boots!"

I had never thought of being ashamed of my hands before; but I began to consider them a very indifferent pair. Her contempt for me was so strong, that it became infectious, and I caught it.

She won the game, and I dealt. I misdealt, as was only natural, when I knew
95 she was lying in wait for me to do wrong; and she denounced me for a stupid,
clumsy labouring-boy.

"You say nothing of her," remarked Miss Havisham to me, as she looked on.
"She says many hard things of you, but you say nothing of her. What do you
think of her?"

100 "I don't like to say," I stammered.

"Tell me in my ear," said Miss Havisham, bending down.

"I think she is very proud," I replied, in a whisper.

"Anything else?"

"I think she is very pretty."

105 "Anything else?"

"I think she is very insulting." (She was looking at me then with a look of
supreme aversion.)

"Anything else?"

"I think I should like to go home."

110 "And never see her again, though she is so pretty?"

"I am not sure that I shouldn't like to see her again, but I should like to go
home now."

"You shall go soon," said Miss Havisham, aloud. "Play the game out."

Saving for the one weird smile at first, I should have felt almost sure that Miss
115 Havisham's face could not smile. It had dropped into a watchful and brooding
expression – most likely when all the things about her had become transfixed –
and it looked as if nothing could ever lift it up again. Her chest had dropped, so
that she stooped; and her voice had dropped, so that she spoke low, and with a
dead lull upon her; altogether, she had the appearance of having drooped, body
120 and soul, within and without, under the weight of a crushing blow.

I played the game to an end with Estella, and she beggared me. She threw the
cards down on the table when she had won them all, as if she despised them for
having been won of me.

"When shall I have you here again?" said Miss Havisham. "Let me think."

125 I was beginning to remind her that today was Wednesday, when she checked
me with her former impatient movement of the fingers of her right hand.

"There, there! I know nothing of days of the week; I know nothing of weeks
of the year. Come again after six days. You hear?"

"Yes, ma'am."

130 "Estella, take him down. Let him have something to eat, and let him roam and
look about him while he eats. Go, Pip."

I followed the candle down, as I had followed the candle up, and she stood it
in the place where we had found it. Until she opened the side entrance, I had
fancied, without thinking about it, that it must necessarily be night-time. The
135 rush of the daylight quite confounded me, and made me feel as if I had been in
the candlelight of the strange room many hours.

"You are to wait here, you boy," said Estella; and disappeared and closed the door.

I took the opportunity of being alone in the courtyard, to look at my coarse
hands and my common boots. My opinion of those accessories was not
140 favourable. They had never troubled me before, but they troubled me now, as
vulgar appendages. I determined to ask Joe why he had ever taught me to call
those picture-cards, Jacks, which ought to be called knaves. I wished Joe had

been rather more genteelly brought up, and then I should have been so too.

145 　　She came back, with some bread and meat and a little mug of beer. She put the mug down on the stones of the yard, and gave me the bread and meat without looking at me, as insolently as if I were a dog in disgrace. I was so humiliated, hurt, spurned, offended, angry, sorry – I cannot hit upon the right name for the smart – God knows what its name was – that tears started to my eyes. The moment they sprang there, the girl looked at me with a quick delight in
150 having been the cause of them. This gave me power to keep them back and to look at her: so she gave a contemptuous toss – but with a sense, I thought, of having made too sure that I was so wounded – and left me.

　　But, when she was gone, I looked about me for a place to hide my face in, and got behind one of the gates in the brewery-lane, and leaned my sleeve against the
155 wall there, and leaned my forehead on it and cried. As I cried, I kicked the wall, and took a hard twist at my hair; so bitter were my feelings, and so sharp was the smart without a name, that needed counteraction.

The following questions will help you to gather your thoughts about the story of Miss Havisham. Before you begin, you may wish to remind yourself of the techniques writers use in their work to affect the way readers feel.

Charlotte Rampling as Miss Havisham in a film of the novel made in 1999.

1 Give at least two reasons why Pip feels so uncomfortable during this visit.

2 What do you think may be the full explanation for Miss Havisham's strange behaviour? Look at:

▶ the setting

▶ the way she looks

▶ information she gives Pip

▶ what she says to Estella

▶ the tone of what she says.

3 Why does Pip find it so hard to please Miss Havisham? Think about:

▶ his feelings

▶ the situation in which he finds himself.

4 What have you learned about Estella from this extract? Give evidence to support your views. Think about:

▶ the way she is described

▶ the way she behaves

▶ the tone of what she says.

5 In separate paragraphs of up to 50 words each, describe how Dickens presents the characters of:

a) Pip

b) Estella

c) Miss Havisham.

Discuss your answers with the rest of your class.

Development

Now that you have clarified your views about the characters, you are going to work out how Dickens uses skillful devices to influence the way you think about them.

Printed below are several statements about the passage you have read. Working in a group, you will be responsible for one of these statements. You should:

a) decide whether you agree with the statement

b) collect evidence from the extract to support your view

c) ensure that you use the terminology you have learned from the writer's toolbox when reacting to the statements.

Statements

▶ The setting of this extract is important to our understanding of the events and the characters.

▶ The fact that the story is told by Pip is not important.

▶ The opening paragraphs engage the readers' interest and are vital in helping us to realise that the old lady is unusual.

▶ The way the characters talk to each other is not a feature of any importance in this extract.

▶ The final two paragraphs of the extract are vital in building up sympathy for Pip.

▶ The description of the events in this extract help the reader to form a vivid impression of Pip, Miss Havisham and Estella.

▶ Dickens' choice of vocabulary, sentence structure and punctuation help us to gain a better understanding of the characters involved.

Nominate one person from your group to present the statement you have analysed and to explain your reaction to it.

Review

What have you learned about:

▶ Miss Havisham?

▶ Estella?

▶ the social system in Dickens time?

Assignment Watch

In this Step, you have seen what a difficult and highly eccentric person Miss Havisham is, especially to a young boy like Pip. Dickens has created this impression by the way he has used the devices listed in the tool kit. The notes that you have made and the examples you have found will be useful when you tackle the assignment.

You have also learned of the way that Pip has become aware of social status for the first time and has become conscious that he has little chance of rising above this status.

Step 4 – Dialogue

In this Step, you are going to look more closely at how writers use dialogue in their work.

You Need to Know

Dickens was renowned for his ability to reproduce the dialogue he heard around him. The voices in Dickens' novels are distinctive – the lower and middle classes are captured in a particularly accurate and memorable way. He was also a very skilful mimic, able to impersonate voices at will.

It is also to be remembered that he was a parliamentary reporter before he became a novelist. This job involved writing down the speeches of the politicians for publication in the newspapers. To do this job, he had to learn what is known as 'shorthand' (a system of rapid handwriting, using symbols to represent words or phrases). His use of phonetic spelling led him to listen very carefully to the sounds of words. In this way, he was able to reproduce the speech he heard around him accurately.

Dickens was also a keen walker of the streets and was a keen observer of the scenes of daily life. In his biography of Dickens, Peter Ackroyd notes:

"There were the street conjurors, the acrobats…and the glee singers; and there were all the cries of London, 'Chestnuts all ott!', 'Half a quire of paper for a penny', 'An aypenny the lot!', amid the shouts of the people themselves. So when we wonder at the quirkiness that springs from the mouths of Dickens' characters, we ought to remember that this was a period in which the colour and originality of London speech would have been taken for granted. When the nature of Dickensian caricature and dialogue is considered, it is wise to remember the rich tumult of voices from which it sprang and encircled him as he walked through the crowded thoroughfares."

Accurately recreating the voices he heard around him, Dickens is able to give his characters real depth, and not just through his descriptions of their actions and physical appearance. By reproducing their speech, he allows the characters to describe themselves to the reader.

A busy London street in Victorian times.

Starting Point

In small groups, discuss the three questions below and be prepared to feed back your ideas to the class.

1 What can you tell about a person from the way in which they speak?

2 What assumptions might people make when they hear a particular accent?

3 What other factors do people consider when listening to speech (for example the vocabulary used, the speed of delivery, etc.)?

Moving On

The way in which people speak and the words they use tell us about their background and education. Writers use dialogue or speech for several reasons, for example:

▶ to pass on information to the reader so that the story is clear

▶ to pass on details about characters who are not involved at that point in the story, but who are important to the plot as a whole

▶ to show us something about the speaker's personality.

For this purpose, it is important to look first at the four most common types of sentence that we use in speech. Read the following explanations. Note anything about this you don't understand.

Statements

These are sentences that give us some information.

My book is still at home.
Spain is a popular place for a holiday.

Key Concept

The tone or stress with which you say something can have a considerable impact on your intended meaning and how it is received by the listener. Similarly, a writer can affect the 'tone' in direct speech or dialogue by using particular types of sentences and vocabulary. This helps the reader to understand something about the character's mood and personality.

1 *"Get out!" she snapped. "You have gone too far this time."*

The word 'snapped' suggests anger and the speaker, by her use of an imperative (Get out!), is showing force and authority in her speech.

2 *"Would you like to sit by the window? The view is so lovely from there."*

The use of a question and statement combine here to show the speaker's consideration towards the other person. If this is typical, then the speaker is well mannered and courteous.

Questions

These sentences require an answer.

Have you seen my tie?
What would you like for your dinner?

Imperatives or commands

These are sentences that give instructions or commands.

Turn left at the next junction.
Come here.

Exclamations

These are sentences that are said with a strong emphasis, often suggesting a deep excitement or alarm.

You made me jump!
We're in trouble now!

Development

You looked briefly at how Magwitch speaks in Step 2. You are now going to examine the speech used by Miss Havisham, Pip, Estella and Magwitch, and further discuss what it suggests about the speaker.

1 Read the dialogue spoken by one of the following in the first two extracts:

a) Pip

b) Estella

c) Miss Havisham

d) Magwitch.

2 Discuss and make notes on:

▶ the types of sentences used

▶ the speaker's tone

▶ the ways in which Dickens conveys the ways in which his characters speak

▶ what these tell the reader about your chosen character.

Remember to note down examples to support your views.

You are now going to share your thoughts with the rest of the class. In particular, you should make clear:

▶ what the dialogue tells the reader about the speaker

▶ how the speaker's dialogue affects the way the reader reacts to him or her.

Prepare your notes for presentation to the class.

▶ List the points you wish to make.

▶ List the evidence which supports your views.

▶ Decide on the form of your presentation. You may wish to use OHTs, a flip chart, Powerpoint, lists, spidergrams, etc.

▶ Decide on the role of each person in your presentation.

Present your findings to the class. Be sure to support your opinions with evidence.

Review

1 What have you learned about:

▶ different types of sentence?

▶ Miss Havisham, Pip, Magwitch and Estella?

▶ how writers use dialogue?

2 How does tone influence the way we feel about characters?

Assignment Watch

In this Step, you have examined the way in which dialogue can deepen the readers' understanding of character and situation. You will be required to comment on these devices from the tool kit in tackling your assignment. The notes you have made will help you in doing this.

Step 5 – Wemmick and the Aged

Starting Point

It is very important that when you read *Great Expectations* you bear in mind what it must have been like to live in nineteenth-century London. It is vital that Dickens' characters are viewed against this backdrop.

You Need to Know

Later in this Step, you will look closely at the character of Wemmick. Wemmick is a clerk working in and around Newgate – a notorious prison in London at the time Dickens was writing. The *Chronicles of Newgate* described what it was like there:

> "Lunatics raving mad ranged up and down the wards, a terror to all they encountered … mock marriages were of constant occurrence … a school and a nursery of crime … the most depraved were free to contaminate and demoralise their more innocent fellows."

Dickens was fascinated by the looming gatehouse of the prison. When he first came to London as a boy, bodies of executed prisoners were still displayed on the walls of Newgate as a deterrent to would-be criminals. There is an account in *Sketches by Boz* in which he contemplates the fact that thousands of people each day "pass and repass this gloomy depository of the guilt and misery of London, in one

The exercise yard at Newgate.

perpetual stream of life and bustle, utterly unmindful of the throng of wretched creatures pent up within it". In *Oliver Twist*, Fagin awaits execution there and Dickens returns to "those dreadful walls of Newgate, which have hidden so much misery and such unspeakable anguish".

It is worth remembering this when you later consider why Wemmick likes to raise the drawbridge and "cut off the communication" with the world outside, as well as why he insists on keeping his work and home life completely separate.

As a class, come up with as many differences (there are literally hundreds) as you can between society today and the society in which Dickens was writing. Two have been done for you. Think about transport, food, employment, sanitation, crime and punishment, etc.

Nineteenth-century England	Society Today
No welfare state	Unemployment benefit
Primitive medical care – high death rates	National Health Service

Moving On

In the early part of this unit, you have been learning about the variety of technical devices available in the writers' tool kit. You are now going to use the knowledge you have gained in your reading of the following extract.

◖Background to the extract◗

At this stage in the novel, Pip is a young man living in London. He is by now making his way in the world and has little contact with the Joe Gargery. He has made the acquaintance of a solicitor, Mr Jaggers, and his eccentric clerk, Wemmick.

Read the following extract, which describes what happens when Pip accepts an invitation to visit the Wemmick household.

Extract 3 – Wemmick and the Aged

Mr Wemmick … gave me to understand that we had arrived in the district of Walworth.

It appeared to be a collection of back lanes, ditches, and little gardens, and to present the aspect of a rather dull retirement. Wemmick's house was a little
5 wooden cottage in the midst of plots of garden, and the top of it was cut out and painted like a battery mounted with guns.

"My own doing," said Wemmick. "Looks pretty; don't it?"

I highly commended it. I think it was the smallest house I ever saw; with the queerest gothic windows (by far the greater part of them sham), and a gothic
10 door, almost too small to get in at.

"That's a real flagstaff, you see," said Wemmick, "and on Sundays I run up a real flag. Then look here. After I have crossed this bridge, I hoist it up – so – and cut off the communication."

The bridge was a plank, and it crossed a chasm about four feet wide and two
15 deep. But it was very pleasant to see the pride with which he hoisted it up and made it fast; smiling as he did so, with a relish and not merely mechanically.

"At nine o'clock every night, Greenwich time," said Wemmick, "the gun fires. There he is, you see! And when you hear him go, I think you'll say he's a Stinger."

The piece of ordnance referred to was mounted in a separate fortress,
20 constructed of lattice-work. It was protected from the weather by an ingenious little tarpaulin contrivance in the nature of an umbrella.

"Then, at the back," said Wemmick, "out of sight, so as not to impede the idea of fortifications – for it's a principle with me, if you have an idea, carry it out and keep it up – I don't know whether that's your opinion – "
25 I said, decidedly.

"At the back, there's a pig, and there are fowls and rabbits; then I knock together my own little frame, you see, and grow cucumbers; and you'll judge at supper what sort of a salad I can raise. So, sir," said Wemmick, smiling again, but seriously too, as he shook his head, "If you can suppose the little place besieged,
30 it would hold out a devil of a time in point of provisions."

Then he conducted me to a bower about a dozen yards off, but which was approached by such ingenious twists of path that it took quite a long time to get at; and in this retreat our glasses were already set forth. Our punch was cooling in an ornamental lake, on whose margin the bower was raised. This piece of
35 water (with an island in the middle which might have been the salad for supper) was of a circular form, and he had constructed a fountain in it, which, when you

set a little mill going and took a cork out of a pipe, played to that powerful extent that it made the back of your hand quite wet.

40 "I am my own engineer, and my own carpenter, and my own plumber, and my own gardener, and my own Jack of all Trades," said Wemmick, in acknowledging my compliments. "Well; it's a good thing, you know. It brushes the Newgate cobwebs away, and pleases the Aged. You wouldn't mind being at once introduced to the Aged, would you? It wouldn't put you out?"

45 I expressed the readiness I felt, and we went into the Castle. There we found, sitting by a fire, a very old man in a flannel coat; clean, cheerful, comfortable, and well cared for, but intensely deaf.

"Well, aged parent," said Wemmick, shaking hands with him in a cordial and jocose way, "how are you?"

"All right, John; all right!" replied the old man.

50 "Here's Mr Pip, aged parent," said Wemmick, "and I wish you could hear his name. – Nod away at him, Mr Pip; that's what he likes. Nod away at him, if you please, like winking!"

"This is a fine place of my son's, sir," cried the old man, while I nodded as hard as I possibly could. "This is a pretty pleasure-ground, sir. This spot and
55 these beautiful works upon it ought to be kept together by the Nation, after my son's time, for the people's enjoyment."

"You're as proud of it as Punch; ain't you, Aged?" said Wemmick, contemplating the old man, with his hard face really softened; "there's a nod for you;" giving him a tremendous one; "there's another for you;" giving him a still
60 more tremendous one; "you like that, don't you? If you're not tired, Mr Pip – though I know it's tiring to strangers – will you tip him one more? You can't think how it pleases him."

I tipped him several more, and he was in great spirits. We left him bestirring himself to feed the fowls, and we sat down to our punch in the arbour; where
65 Wemmick told me as he smoked a pipe that it had taken him a good many years to bring the property up to its present pitch of perfection.

"Is it your own, Mr Wemmick?"

"Oh yes," said Wemmick, "I have got hold of it, a bit at a time. It's a freehold, by George!"

70 "Is it, indeed? I hope Mr Jaggers admires it?"

"Never seen it," said Wemmick. "Never heard of it. Never seen the Aged. Never heard of him. No; the office is one thing, and private life is another. When I go into the office, I leave the Castle behind me, and when I come into the Castle, I leave the office behind me. If it's not in any way disagreeable to you,
75 you'll oblige me by doing the same. I don't wish it professionally spoken about."

Of course I felt my good faith involved in the observance of his request. The punch being very nice, we sat there drinking it and talking, until it was almost nine o'clock. "Getting near gun-fire," said Wemmick then, as he laid down his pipe; 'it's the Aged's treat."

80 Proceeding into the Castle again, we found the Aged heating the poker, with expectant eyes, as a preliminary to the performance of this great nightly ceremony. Wemmick stood with his watch in his hand, until the moment was come for him to take the red-hot poker from the Aged, and repair to the battery.

85 He took it, and went out, and presently the Stinger went off with a Bang that shook the crazy little box of a cottage as if it must fall to pieces, and made every glass and teacup in it ring. Upon this, the Aged – who I believe would have been blown out of his arm-chair but for holding on by the elbows – cried out exultingly, "He's fired! I heerd him!" and I nodded at the old gentleman until it is no figure of speech to declare that I absolutely could not see him.

The following questions will help you to gather your thoughts on this extract. Note down your responses.

1 What evidence is there that Wemmick is proud of his achievements?

2 Judging from the aspects of his home he chooses to show off, what do you think are the most important things in Wemmick's life?

3 Why do you think his employer, Mr Jaggers, has not been told about Wemmick's home?

4 How does Wemmick feel about Pip? Give evidence to support your views.

5 How does Pip feel about Wemmick?

6 Pip cannot resist pointing out the humour in this situation. Find two examples from this episode that Pip finds amusing.

An illustration from the 1885 edition showing Wemmick, Pip and The Aged.

Discuss your answers with the rest of the class.

Development

You are going to work in groups to explore this extract more closely.

First, you will work with two other people to discuss what you have learned about Pip, Wemmick and the Aged. This will be your "home" group.

Next, each member of your home group will join with others to focus on one character. These groups will become "experts" on one character.

Finally, the home groups will meet again to share what they learned from their expert groups.

1 Discuss the points below –

The impressions you have of each of the three characters involved: Pip; Wemmick; The Aged.

What kind of people are they?

Think about:

▶ Social standing

▶ Sense of family

▶ Age

▶ The way they behave towards each other

▶ The way Wemmick thinks about his home and working life.

▶ Are they likeable characters? Why?

2 How does Dickens influence the impressions you have and arouse feelings and reactions in the reader? Refer to the Writers' Tool-kit on page 53.

3 Now decide which character you will be responsible for and make notes of your discussion points to use in the "expert" group.

Join the members of the other groups who have worked on the same character as you. You will now act as experts on your chosen character.

Share your original (Home) group's thinking about your character with your new partners (Expert Group).

Compile a full set of notes to include all the points and supporting evidence that you have discussed.

You should look back at the notes your group made under the headings given in number 1 above.

Return to your home group and report back what you learned from the expert group.

Review

What have you learned about the characters of Pip, Wemmick and The Aged?

Assignment Watch

In this Step, you have examined the way Dickens presents the characters of Wemmick and the Aged through the eyes of Pip.

You should now understand the importance of the social and historical background to the novel, and be able to view the peculiarities of Wemmick's life and character against what you know of what it would have been like to live in this time.

Step 6 – Collecting Your Thoughts

You have analysed three extracts from *Great Expectations* in which Pip meets three characters whose lives are clearly unusual – Magwitch, Miss Havisham and Wemmick.

You should now be able to gather your thoughts about the techniques and devices Dickens uses to build our understanding, sympathy, amusement and even our support for some of the characters in his books.

Later in this Step you are going to present your work to the rest of the class.

Starting Point

Share your ideas about what you need to include to make a successful presentation. Two ideas have been suggested on the spidergram below. How many of your own can you add?

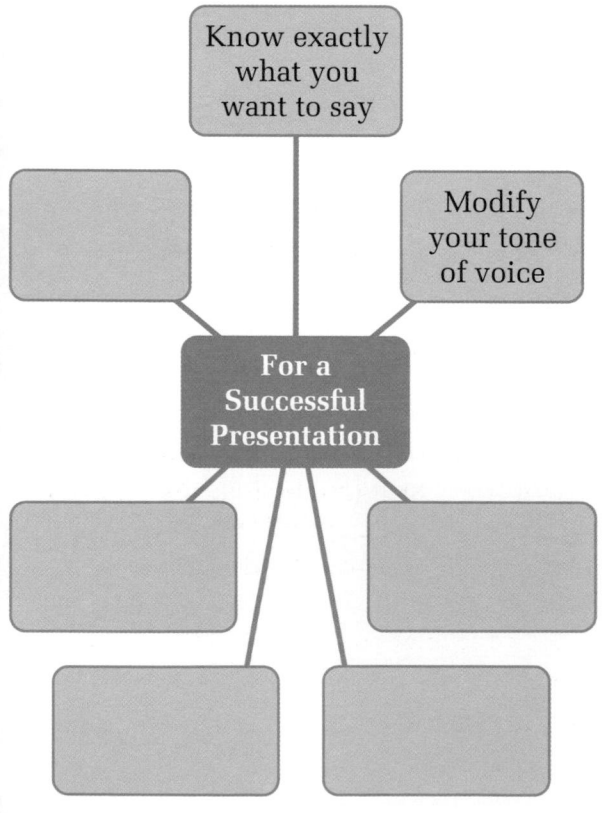

Know exactly what you want to say

Modify your tone of voice

For a Successful Presentation

Moving On

1 Your group should take responsibility for one of the following devices:

▶ Setting

▶ Dialogue

▶ Voice

2 Organise the points you have collected from the previous Steps into a presentation to the rest of the class. The following prompts may help you. Make sure that you look back at the 'You Need to Know' boxes as these may help you give depth to your answers.

Setting

▶ Do the three different settings create an appropriate atmosphere for the events in the extracts? Find evidence to support your opinion.

▶ Collect words and phrases that Dickens uses to create vivid settings.

▶ What effect do these settings have on the reader?

▶ How do the graveyard, the old house and Wemmick's home add to your understanding of how the characters think and feel?

▶ How does Dickens' use of setting suit the characters he places in them? Do these surroundings increase your sympathy for the characters?

Dialogue

▶ Collect examples of the way each character speaks to others.

▶ What tone do the characters use towards others?

▶ What does their speech reveal of their personality, social status, education and attitude to others?

▶ How does the way the characters speak affect the way you feel about them?

▶ How does Dickens' use of dialogue enable the reader to understand the characters he creates more fully? Does this skill allow the readers to sympathise with the characters?

Voice

Great Expectations is written using a first-person narrative structure, with Pip acting as the narrator.

▶ How does this style help the reader to understand the events, Pip himself, and the other characters involved? Collect seven examples from the text to support your views.

▶ What are the advantages to Dickens of using this method of story telling?

▶ Are there any disadvantages?

▶ How does Dickens' use of the first-person narrator enable readers to sympathise with Pip? What are the main benefits of writing in this way?

Development

1 Prepare a presentation to the rest of the group.

▶ List the points you would like to make.

▶ List the evidence you would like to use.

▶ Decide on the form of your presentation, e.g. list, spidergram, table, flip chart, OHT, etc.

▶ Decide on the role of each person in your presentation.

2 Make your presentation to the rest of the class. You should aim to talk for three to five minutes.

Make notes on the presentations made by other groups. You could set out your notes in table form, as follows:

Device	Effect	Evidence

Review

What have you learned about the way Dickens uses setting, dialogue and voice?

Assignment Watch

In this Step, you have examined Dickens' use of a variety of devices to influence the way readers respond to characters and their circumstances. Your understanding of *how* he does this is a key element in the assignment for this unit. Your notes should provide you with an invaluable source of examples and comments to support your answer.

Step 7 Tackling the Assignment

You are now ready to start thinking about the work you will be expected to complete for GCSE coursework. This page contains three assignments based on *Great Expectations*.

Starting Point

Choose the assignment about which you feel most confident.

Assignment 1

1 In the extract where Pip, a boy from a very humble background meets Miss Havisham, a rich but eccentric lady, Dickens wants the reader to feel sympathetic towards Pip. How does he make us feel this way?

Assignment 2

2 How does Dickens create sympathy for his characters in Great Expectations? Focus on Pip and one or two other characters you have studied.

Assignment 3

3 How does Dickens create characters that are both memorable and striking? Make sure that you refer to at least three.

Moving On

Discuss with other students how to use the following information to help you to plan your assignment.

Planning the assignment:		
Assignment	**Thinking:**	**Structure:**
1	This assignment focuses on the character of Pip as shown in one of the extracts, but you need to look at the way the other characters affect him. The most important part of the question involves the way Dickens makes the reader feel about Pip and how he uses the techniques or devices to achieve that effect. Look at the notes you have made on: ▶ the setting of the piece; the way each character speaks ▶ the way Miss Havisham and Pip are separated by social class ▶ the mood of the piece ▶ the use of Pip as a narrator ▶ the opening and ending of the extract. (Look at the 'Key Concepts'.)	Look again at the notes you have made for this scene. In your response, make sure that you: ▶ explain the purpose and aims of your writing ▶ refer briefly to how the characters have come to meet, their differing social backgrounds and why this is important ▶ comment on the setting and how Miss Havisham's house is likely to seem to Pip ▶ examine the characters of Miss Havisham and Estella. Look at the way they treat Pip in general and especially the way they speak to him ▶ state if you think Dickens is successful in making the reader feel sympathetic towards Pip ▶ use extracts from the text to back up what you say.

Planning the assignment:		
Assignment	**Thinking:**	**Structure:**
2	This assignment allows you look at Pip as he is presented across all three extracts, and to combine the way in which he is presented with the presentation of at least one other character. However, the key to this question is the techniques Dickens uses to arouse sympathy. Treat each character separately and comment on the techniques used in each case. Look at your notes on: ▶ the characters' dialogue ▶ how they are described ▶ the use of Pip as narrator ▶ the setting of each extract ▶ the attitude of the characters ▶ their social status, the way in which the historical setting reflects the period, e.g. 'hulks', 'gibbets', etc.	In your response, make sure that you: ▶ explain the aims and purposes of your writing ▶ use at least two extracts in examining Pip's character to draw evidence to support the comments you make about how you are made to feel sympathetic towards him ▶ point out the similarities in techniques used by Dickens in examining your other character(s) ▶ explain the impact on the reader of the language used in your examples ▶ comment on how successful Dickens is in building sympathy for the characters you have chosen.
Assignment	**Thinking:**	**Structure:**
3	This question requires you to focus on the techniques Dickens employs to create sympathy and to use characters from all three extracts to support your observations. Your response should be detailed, methodical and analytical. Look at the notes you have made and think about how: ▶ the settings affect your view of the characters ▶ the way the social class system affects the characters involved ▶ the mood created in each piece affects your view of each one ▶ the way characters speak affects your thinking about them ▶ the way the historical background informs your understanding of the characters and the setting ▶ the use of Pip as a narrator affects your opinion of characters.	In your response, explain your purpose and decide which characters you are going to focus on. Make sure that you discuss the points below, using the text to back up your arguments where relevant: ▶ the characters physical surroundings and the mood created by the setting ▶ the way they are described ▶ how your knowledge of their social and historical background helps you to better understand them ▶ the way that they speak and what this adds to your understanding of them ▶ whether the techniques Dickens makes use of generate sympathy or comedy (or perhaps both).

Development

Now work with others who have chosen the same assignment.

Use your preliminary notes and the bullet points in the 'Thinking' section of the Assignment breakdown to help you to develop the plan for your assignment.

Review

1 What have learned about the requirements of these assignments?

2 What have you learned about planning a Literature response?

A recent adaptation of the novel (from 1997) starred Ethan Hawke and Gyneth Paltrow in the roles of Pip and Estella. The story was moved to New York.

Step 1 – The Strange Case of Dr Jekyll and Mr Hyde

The story of Jekyll and Hyde has remained very popular since it was written over a century ago. Like *Dracula* and *Frankenstein*, *The Strange Case of Dr Jekyll and Mr Hyde* has been adapted for both television and film. There are many people who have heard of the novel and think they know what it is about – without having actually read it!

In this part of the unit, you are going to consider the idea of a Jekyll and Hyde personality and then explore the first five paragraphs of the novel.

Starting Point

Answer the following questions and be prepared to feedback your answers to the class.

1 If someone is described as having a Jekyll and Hyde personality, what do you think it means? Write a one sentence definition for the expression.

Feedback your ideas to the class. Agree a class definition. Amend your notes as appropriate.

2 Name five characters from film, T.V. or other media that fulfil the definition.

Use the grid below to set out features of the two "sides" of one of the characters you have chosen.

'Normal' personality	'Other' personality
Norman Osborn	The Green Goblin

Feedback your ideas to the rest of the class.

You Need to Know

Robert Louis Stevenson was brought up in Edinburgh and came from a strict religious background. Although he eventually rebelled against the stern and proper Calvinist beliefs of his father, the themes of 'sin' and 'evil' are easy to see in *The Strange Case of Jekyll and Hyde*.

When he was a child growing up in Edinburgh, Stevenson would have been familiar with the story of Deacon Brodie, who was a cabinet maker by day and a criminal by night. This kind of double life may well have affected his portrayal of Dr Jekyll. While his Calvinist upbringing would have taught him to beware of the devil and avoid sinfulness, Stevenson sees the devil as within everybody.

Stevenson held strong views on good and bad conduct and believed that everyone is capable of evil. He believed that evil is just as much a part of human nature as good is. The evil Mr Hyde is part of the respectable Dr Jekyll. At the time the story was published in 1885 although the novel was a success, people found the fact shocking.

A poster from the 1931 film adaptation.

Moving On

Now read the first three paragraphs of the novel.

Mr. Utterson the lawyer was a man of a rugged countenance, that was never lighted by a smile; cold, scanty and embarrassed in discourse; backward in sentiment; lean, long, dusty, dreary, and yet somehow lovable. At friendly meetings, and when the wine was to
5 his taste, something eminently human beaconed from his eye; something indeed which never found its way into his talk, but which spoke not only in these silent symbols of the after-dinner face, but more often and loudly in the acts of his life. He was austere with himself; drank gin when he was alone, to mortify a
10 taste for vintages; and though he enjoyed the theatre, had not crossed the doors of one for twenty years. But he had an approved tolerance for others; sometimes wondering, almost with envy, at the high pressure of spirits involved in their misdeeds; and in any extremity inclined to help rather than to reprove.

15 "I incline to, Cain's heresy," he used to say quaintly. "I let my brother go to the devil in his own way." In this character, it was frequently his fortune to be the last reputable acquaintance and the last good influence in the lives of down-going men. And to such as these, so long as they came about his chambers, he never
20 marked a shade of change in his demeanour.

No doubt the feat was easy to Mr. Utterson; for he was undemonstrative at the best, and even his friendship seemed to be founded in a similar catholicity of good-nature. It is the mark of a modest man to accept his friendly circle ready-made from the
25 hands of opportunity; and that was the lawyer's way. His friends were those of his own blood or those whom he had known the longest; his affections, like ivy, were the growth of time, they implied no aptness in the object. Hence, no doubt, the bond that united him to Mr. Richard Enfield, his distant kinsman, the well-
30 known man about town. It was a nut to crack for many, what these two could see in each other, or what subject they could find in common. It was reported by those who encountered them in their Sunday walks, that they said nothing, looked singularly dull, and would hail with obvious relief the appearance of a friend. For
35 all that, the two men put the greatest store by these excursions, counted them the chief jewel of each week, and not only set aside occasions of pleasure, but even resisted the calls of business, that they might enjoy them uninterrupted.

countenance: face
discourse: speech

austere: strict
vintages: good quality wines

reprove: speak disapprovingly
incline to: believe in
heresy: a belief that is generally thought to be wrong
demeanour: the way a person behaves towards others

catholicity: liberality

aptness: suitability

singularly: remarkably
greatest store: highest importance

Answer the following questions and keep a record of your work.

N.B. you will find a dictionary/thesaurus useful for this activity.

About Mr Utterson

1 Look at the first sentence. Pick out seven words/phrases that describe Mr Utterson's appearance or personality. Discuss what these words suggest about the sort of person he is.

2 Look up the meaning of "eminently" as used in the second sentence. Give another word that could replace it in the sentence without altering its sense or meaning.

3 Look up the meaning of "mortify" and "austere" as used in the third sentence, and "approve" and "reprove" as used in the fourth sentence.

4 In paragraph two, Stevenson says that Utterson is often the last friendly face for "down-going" men. What does he mean by, "I let my brother go to the devil in his own way?"

About Mr Enfield

5 Enfield is described as a "well-known man about town". What does this suggest about his personality?

About them both

6 How did the two men appear to other people when they were out on their walks?

7 How did Utterson think of their time together?

8 "*It was a nut to crack* for many, what these two could see in each other, or what subject they could find in common."

a) What do you think the phrase in italics means?

b) What does the sentence suggest about the way people see the two men?

Share your answers with the rest of the class. Amend your notes as appropriate.

Development

Now you are going to look more closely at the character of Mr Utterson.

1 "Something eminently human beaconed from his eye" when he is able to relax with friends. What does this tell you about his eyes at other times?

2 What do you think is meant by the term "eminently human"?

3 This "human" aspect never finds its way into his talk. What does this tell you about his conversation?

4 We learn that although Utterson is "lean, long, dusty and dreary", he is also somehow "lovable". From what you know about his character, why do you think people might find him lovable? What qualities does he possess?

5 Based on what you have learned from the first two paragraphs, prepare a summary of Utterson's character to feed back to the rest of your class.

Review

What have you learned about:

A "Jekyll and Hyde" personality?
Mr. Utterson?
Mr. Enfield?

Assignment Watch

The way in which characters are presented in the novel is something that needs to be examined very carefully. If you are able to look in detail at the language Stevenson uses to do this, it will stand you in good stead when you come to answer the assignment questions.

Step 2 – Secrets and Reputations

In this Step, you are going to read and analyse the remainder of the opening chapter of the novel in which the character of Mr Hyde is introduced to the reader.

Starting Point

Answer the following questions.

1 List five things about yourself that you would be prepared to share with anyone.

2 What kinds of things do you think people would prefer to keep private? Give reasons for your answer.

3 Can you think of any famous people who have has their private lives exposed by the press? How do you think this has affected their reputations?

Feedback your thoughts to the rest of the class.

Moving On

You are now going to read about an incident witnessed by Enfield when he was returning home late one night.

Mr. Enfield and the lawyer were on the other side of the by-street; but when they came abreast of the entry, the former lifted up his cane and pointed.

"Did you ever remark that door?" he asked; and when his companion had replied in the affirmative, "It is connected in my mind," added he, "with a

5 very odd story."

"Indeed?" said Mr. Utterson, with a slight change of voice, "and what was that?"

"Well, it was this way," returned Mr. Enfield: "I was coming home from some place at the end of the world, about three o' clock of a black winter morning, and my way lay through a part of town where there was literally

10 nothing to be seen but lamps. Street after street, and all the folks asleep — street after street, all lighted up as if for a procession and all as empty as a church — till at last I got into that state of mind when a man listens and listens and begins to long for the sight of a policeman. All at once, I saw two figures: one a little man who was stumping along eastward at a good

15 walk, and the other a girl of maybe eight or ten who was running as hard as she was able down a cross street. Well, sir, the two ran into one another naturally enough at the corner; and then came the horrible part of the thing; for the man trampled calmly over the, child's body and left her screaming on the ground. It sounds nothing to hear, but it was hellish to

20 see. It wasn't like a man; it was like some damned Juggernaut. I gave a view-halloa, took to my heels, collared my gentleman, and brought him back to where there was already quite a group about the screaming child. He was perfectly cool and made no resistance, but gave me one look, so ugly that it brought out the sweat on me like running. The people who had

25 turned out were the girl's own family; and pretty soon, the doctor, for

> **affirmative:** confirming something as true

> **Juggernaut:** any terrible force
> **view-halloa:** shout

whom she had been sent, put in his appearance. Well, the child was not much the worse, more frightened, according to the Sawbones; and there you might have supposed would be an end to it. But there was one curious circumstance. I had taken a loathing to my gentleman at first sight. So had the child's family, which was only natural. But the doctor's case was what struck me. He was the usual cut-and-dry apothecary, of no particular age and colour, with a strong Edinburgh accent, and about as emotional as a bagpipe. Well, sir, he was like the rest of us; every time he looked at my prisoner, I saw that Sawbones turn sick and white with the desire to kill him. I knew what was in his mind, just as he knew what was in mine; and killing being out of the question, we did the next best. We told the man we could and would make such a scandal out of this, as should make his name stink from one end of London to the other. If he had any friends or any credit, we undertook that he should lose them. And all the time, as we were pitching it in red hot, we were keeping the women off him as best we could, for they were as wild as harpies. I never saw a circle of such hateful faces; and there was the man in the middle, with a kind of black, sneering coolness — frightened too, I could see that — but carrying it off, sir, really like Satan. 'If you choose to make capital out of this accident,' said he, 'I am naturally helpless. No gentleman but wishes to avoid a scene,' says he. 'Name your figure.' Well, we screwed him up to a hundred pounds for the child's family; he would have clearly liked to stick out; but there was something about the lot of us that meant mischief, and at last he struck. The next thing was to get the money; and where do you think he carried us but to that place with the door? — whipped out a key, went in, and presently came back with the matter of ten pounds in gold and a cheque for the balance on Coutts's, drawn payable to bearer and signed with a name that I can't mention, though it's one of the points of my story, but it was a name at least very well known and often printed. The figure was stiff; but the signature was good for more than that, if it was only genuine. I took the liberty of pointing out to my gentleman that the whole business looked apocryphal, and that a man does not, in real life, walk into a cellar door at four in the morning and come out of it with another man's cheque for close upon a hundred pounds. But he was quite easy and sneering. 'Set your mind at rest,' says he, 'I will stay with you till the banks open and cash the cheque myself.'

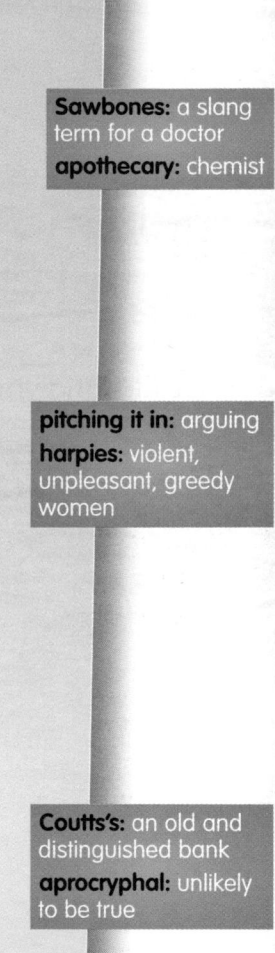

Sawbones: a slang term for a doctor
apothecary: chemist

pitching it in: arguing
harpies: violent, unpleasant, greedy women

Coutts's: an old and distinguished bank
aprocryphal: unlikely to be true

Line numbers: 30, 35, 40, 45, 50, 50, 55

1 As a "man about town", where do you think Enfield is likely to have been until three o'clock in the morning?

2 What kind of night was it?

3 Why do you think the young girl was out on the streets at such a late hour?

4 What happened between the young girl and Hyde?

5 How did Enfield react to what he saw?

6 How did Enfield feel about Hyde?

7 How did the Doctor and the women react to Hyde?

8 Why would Hyde feel threatened when Enfield says, "We told the man we could and would make such a scandal out of this …"?

9 Was Enfield justified in blackmailing Hyde in order to keep the incident secret?

10 What puzzled Enfield about the cheque he was given?

11 What more do we learn about Enfield from this reading?

12 What do we learn about the character of Hyde?

Share your responses with the rest of the class.

Development

The following extract completes Enfield's story.

Read the extract and then answer the questions on page 88.

So we all set off, the doctor, and the child's father, and our friend and myself, and passed the rest of the night in my chambers; and next day, when we had breakfasted, went in a body to the bank. I gave in the cheque myself, and said I had every reason to believe it was a forgery.
5 Not a bit of it. The cheque was genuine."

"Tut-tut," said Mr. Utterson.

"I see you feel as I do," said Mr. Enfield. "Yes, it's a bad story. For my man was a fellow that nobody could have to do with, a really damnable man; and the person that drew the cheque is the very pink of the
10 proprieties, celebrated too, and (what makes it worse) one of your fellows who do what they call good. Black-mail, I suppose; an honest man paying through the nose for some of the capers of his youth. Black-Mail House is what I call that place with the door, in consequence. Though even that, you know, is far from explaining all,"
15 he added, and with the words fell into a vein of musing.

From this he was recalled by Mr. Utterson asking rather suddenly:" And you don't know if the *drawer* of the cheque lives there?"

"A likely place, isn't it?" returned Mr. Enfield. "But I happen to have noticed his address; he lives in some square or other."

20 "And you never asked about the — place with the door?" said Mr. Utterson.

"No, sir: I had a delicacy," was the reply. "I feel very strongly about putting questions; it partakes too much of the style of the day of judgement. You start a question, and it's like starting a stone. You sit
25 quietly on the top of a hill; and away the stone goes, starting others; and presently some bland old bird (the last you would have thought of) is knocked on the head in his own back-garden and the family have to change their name. No, sir, I make it a rule of mine: the more it looks like Queer Street, the less I ask."

30 " A very good rule, too," said the lawyer.

"But I have studied the place for myself," continued Mr. Enfield." It seems scarcely a house. There is no other door, and nobody goes in or out of that one but, once in a great while, the gentleman of my

the properties: standards of behaviour considered correct by polite society

vein of musing: deep thought

had a delicacy: was tactful

day of judgement: doomsday

Queer Street: to have financial difficulties

adventure. There are three windows looking on the court on the first
floor; none below; the windows are always shut but they're clean. And
then there is a chimney which is generally smoking; so somebody must
live there. And yet it's not so sure; for the buildings are so packed
together about that court, that it's hard to say where one ends and
another begins."

The pair walked on again for a while in silence; and then, "Enfield,"
said Mr. Utterson, "that's a good rule of yours."

"Yes, I think it is," returned Enfield.

"But for all that," continued the lawyer, "there's one point I want to
ask: I want to ask the name of that man who walked over the child."

"Well," said Mr. Enfield, "I can't see what harm it would do. It was a
man of the name of Hyde."

"H'm," said Mr. Utterson. "What sort of a man is he to see?"

"He is not easy to describe. There is something wrong with his
appearance; something displeasing, something downright detestable. I
never saw a man I so disliked, and yet I scarce know why. He must be
deformed somewhere; he gives a strong feeling of deformity, although I
couldn't specify the point. He's an extraordinary-looking man, and yet I
really can name nothing out of the way. No, sir; I can make no hand of
it; I can't describe him. And it's not want of memory; for I declare I can
see him this moment."

Mr. Utterson again walked some way in silence and obviously under a
weight of consideration.

"You are sure he used a key?" he inquired at last.

"My dear sir…" began Enfield, surprised out of himself.

"Yes, I know," said Utterson; "I know it must seem
strange. The fact is, if I do not ask you the name of the
other party, it is because I know it already. You see,
Richard, your tale has gone home. If you have been
inexact in any point, you had better correct it."

"I think you might have warned me," returned the other,
with a touch of sullenness. "But I have been pedantically
exact, as you call it. The fellow had a key; and what's
more, he has it still. I saw him use it, not a week ago.

Mr. Utterson sighed deeply but said never a word; and the
young man presently resumed. "Here is another lesson to
say nothing," said he. "I am ashamed of my long tongue.
Let us make a bargain never to refer to this again."

"With all my heart," said the lawyer. "I shake hands on
that, Richard."

downright: utterly

weight of consideration: thinking deeply

pedantically: concerned with small details

John Barrymore as Mr Hyde.

To focus on the extract complete the following sentences quickly by providing an appropriate word.

Enfield believed the cheque to be a _____ but it proved to be genuine.

The cheque was written by someone who was _____ .

Enfield believed that the man who wrote the cheque did so because of _____ .

Utterson and Enfield agree that it is not a good idea to _____ into other people's business.

The man who walked over the child was called _____ .

Utterson and Enfield agree _____ to discuss the incident again.

Share your answers with the rest of the class.

Now you are going to answer some more searching questions on the extract.

1 What is it about the man that makes the others dislike him so much?

2 Find evidence to support the following statements:

i) Utterson and Enfield feel a person's reputation is very important.

ii) The signature on the cheque causes some concern to Enfield.

iii) Utterson and Enfield respect the privacy of people.

iv) Utterson and Enfield are not entirely open with each other.

Share your views with the rest of the class. Amend your notes as appropriate.

Review

What have you learned about:

▷ Mr Hyde?

▷ Mr Utterson?

▷ Mr Enfield?

▷ The importance of privacy/reputation?

▷ The dangers of having your private life exposed?

Assignment Watch

In the first two Steps, you have examined what Stevenson has to say on the subjects of privacy, reputation and how appearances do not always give an exact picture of how people really are. An understanding of the way that appearances can be deceptive in the novel will be important when answering the assignment questions.

Step 3 – *The Carew Murder*

In this Step you will read about one of Mr. Hyde's violent attacks and examine the ways in which other characters react to his behaviour.

Once again, the text needs to be read very closely. This is a novel of secrets and it can be easy to miss important points. In some ways, the reader is like a detective here.

Starting Point

A constant theme in this story is human nature and the inner conflicts it can arouse. At this point, you are going to consider aspects of behaviour that can be described as typical of any person.

1 Set out two columns with the headings Desirable Characteristics and Undesirable Characteristics

2 Under each heading, list appropriate aspects of human nature. The following examples will help you to get started.

Desirable Characteristics	Undesirable Characteristics
kindness generosity honesty	greed laziness hatred

3 Share your thoughts with the rest of the class.

4 Read the following statements about human nature. Choose one with which you strongly agree and one with which you strongly disagree and give reasons for your choices.

▶ People are mostly good and behave well because they want to.

▶ We are all capable of doing very bad things but choose not to for a variety of reasons.

▶ Some people are born evil and have no saving graces.

▶ Some people only do good things to gain a good reputation.

▶ Some people are more concerned about others than they are about themselves.

5 Share your views with the rest of the class. How would you sum up human nature?

Moving On

The following incident describes the death of Sir Danvers Carew, an M.P. murdered by Mr. Hyde one foggy night.

Read the following extract relating to the Carew murder.

Nearly a year later, in the month of October, 18–, London was startled by a crime of singular ferocity and rendered all the more notable by the high position of the victim. The details were few and startling. A maid servant living alone in a house not far from the river, had gone upstairs to bed about eleven. Although a fog
5 rolled over the city in the small hours, the early part of the night was cloudless, and the lane, which the maid's window overlooked, was brilliantly lit by the full moon. It seems she was romantically given, for she sat down upon her box, which stood immediately under the window, and fell into a dream of musing. Never (she used to say, with streaming tears, when she narrated that experience), never had
10 she felt more at peace with all men or thought more kindly of the world. And as she so sat she became aware of an aged beautiful gentleman with white hair, drawing near along the lane; and advancing to meet him, another and very small gentleman, to whom at first she paid less attention. When they had come within speech (which was just under the maid's eyes) the older man bowed and accosted
15 the other with a very pretty manner of politeness. It did not seem as if the subject of his address were of great importance; indeed, from his pointing, it some times appeared as if he were only inquiring his way; but the moon shone on his face as he spoke, and the girl was pleased to watch it, it seemed to breathe such an innocent and old-world kindness of disposition, yet with something high too, as
20 of a well-founded self-content. Presently her eye wandered to the other, and she was surprised to recognise in him a certain Mr. Hyde, who had once visited her master and for whom she had conceived a dislike. He had in his hand a heavy cane, with which he was trifling; but he answered never a word, and seemed to listen with an ill-contained impatience. And then all of a sudden he broke out in a
25 great flame of anger, stamping with his foot, brandishing the cane, and carrying on (as the maid described it) like a madman. The old gentleman took a step back, with the air of one very much surprised and a trifle hurt; and at that Mr. Hyde broke out of all bounds and clubbed him to the earth. And next moment, with ape-like fury, he was trampling his victim under foot and hailing down a storm of
30 blows, under which the bones were audibly shattered and the body jumped upon the roadway. At the horror of these sights and sounds, the maid fainted.

It was two o'clock when she came to herself and called for the police. The murderer was gone long ago; but there lay his victim in the middle of the lane, incredibly mangled. The stick with which the deed had been done, although it
35 was of some rare and very tough and heavy wood, had broken in the middle under the stress of this insensate cruelty; and one splintered half had rolled in the neighbouring gutter—the other, without doubt, had been carried away by the murderer. A purse and gold watch were found upon the victim: but no cards or papers, except a sealed and stamped envelope, which he had been probably
40 carrying to the post, and which bore the name and address of Mr. Utterson.

This was brought to the lawyer the next morning, before he was out of bed; and he had no sooner seen it and been told the circumstances, than he shot out a solemn lip. "I shall say nothing till I have seen the body," said he; "this may be very serious. Have the kindness to wait while I dress." And with the same grave
45 countenance he hurried through his breakfast and drove to the police station,

---

singular: remarkable

romantically given: prone to having ideas that are not realistic

musing: thinking about something for a long time

accosted: came and spoke to

disposition: way of behaving

insensate: senseless

whither the body had been carried. As soon as he came into the cell, he nodded.

whither: where

"Yes," said he, "I recognise him. I am sorry to say that this is Sir Danvers Carew."

"Good God, sir," exclaimed the officer, "is it possible?" And the next moment his eye lighted up with professional ambition. "This will make a deal of noise,"
50 he said. "And perhaps you can help us to the man." And he briefly narrated what the maid had seen, and showed the broken stick.

Mr. Utterson had already quailed at the name of Hyde; but when the stick was laid before him, he could doubt no longer; broken and battered as it was, he recognized it for one that he had himself presented many years before to
55 Henry Jekyll.

quailed: shrunk back

"Is this Mr. Hyde a person of small stature?" he inquired.

"Particularly small and particularly wicked-looking, is what the maid calls him," said the officer.

Mr. Utterson reflected; and then, raising his head, "If you will come with me in
60 my cab," he said, "I think I can take you to his house."

Answer the following questions and keep a record of your responses.

1 List the major events leading up to Carew's murder. You should list no more than 7 points.

2 Why did the police involve Utterson in the incident?

3 Why is it important that Carew's purse and a gold watch were found on his dead body?

4 What did the police officer mean when he said that the murder "will make a deal of noise"?

Share your answers with the rest of the class. Amend your notes if necessary.

Now answer the following questions about the characters and their actions and keep a record of your thoughts and ideas.

a) Find details to show that Hyde's attack appeared to be unprovoked and vicious.

b) Why do the policeman's eyes "light up with professional ambition" when he finds that the murdered man is a well known M.P.?

c) What do you think Mr. Utterson means when he says of the murder, "this may be very serious"? Considering that the man is dead, how much more serious can it get?

d) Why does Utterson not tell the police his suspicions about the murder?

e) What might Sir Danvers Carew have been doing down by the river late at night?

f) Can we trust the maid's testimony? What do we know about her? Look at how many times "seem" and "appear" are used in her story.

g) A letter for Utterson is found on the body of Sir Danvers Carew. Does this tell us anything about him?

Share your thoughts with the rest of the class.

Development

Now read the rest of the chapter

It was by this time about nine in the morning, and the first fog of the season. A great chocolate-coloured pall lowered over heaven, but the wind was continually charging and routing these embattled vapours; so that as the cab crawled from street to street, Mr. Utterson beheld a marvellous
5　number of degrees and hues of twilight; for here it would be dark like the back-end of evening; and there would be a glow of a rich, lurid brown, like the light of some strange conflagration; and here, for a moment, the fog would be quite broken up, and a haggard shaft of daylight would glance in between the swirling wreaths. The dismal quarter of Soho seen under these
10　changing glimpses, with its muddy ways, and slatternly passengers, and its lamps, which had never been extinguished or had been kindled afresh to combat this mournful reinvasion of darkness, seemed, in the lawyer's eyes, like a district of some city in a nightmare. The thoughts of his mind, besides, were of the gloomiest dye; and when he glanced at the companion
15　of his drive, he was conscious of some touch of that terror of the law and the law's officers, which may at times assail the most honest.

As the cab drew up before the address indicated, the fog lifted a little and showed him a dingy street, a gin palace, a low French eating house, a shop for the retail of penny numbers and twopenny salads, many ragged
20　children huddled in the doorways, and many women of many different nationalities passing out, key in hand, to have a morning glass; and the next moment the fog settled down again upon that part, as brown as umber, and cut him off from his blackguardly surroundings. This was the home of Henry Jekyll's favourite; of a man who was heir to a
25　quarter of a million sterling.

An ivory-faced and silvery-haired old woman opened the door. She had an evil face, smoothed by hypocrisy: but her manners were excellent. Yes, she said, this was Mr. Hyde's, but he was not at home; he had been in that night very late, but he had gone away again in less than an hour;
30　there was nothing strange in that; his habits were very irregular, and he was often absent; for instance, it was nearly two months since she had seen him till yesterday.

"Very well, then, we wish to see his rooms," said the lawyer; and when the woman began to declare it was impossible, "I had better tell you who this
35　person is," he added. "This is Inspector Newcomen of Scotland Yard."

A flash of odious joy appeared upon the woman's face. "Ah!" said she, "he is in trouble! What has he done?"

Mr. Utterson and the inspector exchanged glances. "He don't seem a very popular character," observed the latter. "And now, my good woman,
40　just let me and this gentleman have a look about us."

In the whole extent of the house, which but for the old woman remained otherwise empty, Mr. Hyde had only used a couple of rooms;

---

charging and routing these embattled vapours: the wind was blowing the fog around as though fighting it

conflagration: a large, destructive fire

slatternly: dirty untidy (women)

gin palace: a place where cheap (dangerous) gin was sold

penny numbers: cheap books

umber: a brown earth

blackguardly: unprincipled, villainous

favourite: a person regarded with special preference

odious: hideous, hateful

but these were furnished with luxury and good taste. A closet was filled with wine; the plate was of silver, the napery elegant; a good picture
45 hung upon the walls, a gift (as Utterson supposed) from Henry Jekyll, who was much of a connoisseur; and the carpets were of many plies and agreeable in colour. At this moment, however, the rooms bore every mark of having been recently and hurriedly ransacked;

clothes lay about the floor, with their pockets inside out; lock-fast
50 drawers stood open; and on the hearth there lay a pile of grey ashes, as though many papers had been burned. From these embers the inspector disinterred the butt end of a green cheque book, which had resisted the action of the fire; the other half of the stick was found behind the door; and as this clinched his suspicions, the officer declared himself
55 delighted. A visit to the bank, where several thousand pounds were found to be lying to the murderer's credit, completed his gratification.

"You may depend upon it, sir," he told Mr. Utterson: "I have him in my hand. He must have lost his head, or he never would have left the stick or, above all, burned the cheque book. Why, money's life to the man. We have
60 nothing to do but wait for him at the bank, and get out the handbills."

This last, however, was not so easy of accomplishment; for Mr. Hyde had numbered few familiars – even the master of the servant maid had only seen him twice; his family could nowhere be traced; he had never been photographed; and the few who could describe him differed
65 widely, as common observers will. Only on one point were they agreed; and that was the haunting sense of unexpressed deformity with which the fugitive impressed his beholders.

napery: linen

connoisseur: a person with special knowledge and appreciation of a subject

disinterred: dug out

gratification: pleasure

familiars: friends

Read the following statements and find evidence to support them. Keep a record of your responses.

i) Soho is a place of poverty and vice.

ii) Mr. Hyde's maid enjoyed the fact that Mr. Hyde was in trouble.

iii) Mr. Hyde seems to have panicked before escaping.

iv) It would be difficult to track down Mr. Hyde.

v) The policeman is enjoying his job.

Share your responses with the rest of the class.

Review

In this Step, what have you learned about:

▸ Mr. Utterson?

▸ Mr. Hyde?

▸ The police officer?

▸ Mr. Hyde's servant?

▸ Human nature?

Assignment Watch

In this Step you have examined how characters do not always reveal their inner thoughts, even when they have to cope with very serious issues like the murder of another person.

93

Step 4 – Mood and Setting

You Need to Know

The city of London in the novel is presented in a very imprecise way. Stevenson's geographical references are frequently inexact or impossible to follow. Real areas are sometimes mentioned (Soho or Cavendish Square) although other names are invented (Gaunt Street) or described in a way that is extremely vague e.g. Sir Danvers Carew is murdered "not far from the river". London is in this sense an extended metaphor, with good and evil living side by side and very much a part of everyday life.

At the time Stevenson was writing, London was certainly a city of marked contrasts, with its upmarket professional district being very different from its industrial section. London was also a city of fog and pollution, as well as of narrow poorly lit, maze-like streets. Such a setting suits Stevenson's story of shifting identities and hidden truths perfectly. Not only does the fog cover-up the activities of Mr Hyde (and others) but also helps provide the cold, damp, eerie atmosphere of the tale.

Pollution on the Thames – 1858.

Starting Point

Read lines 1–25 from the Carew Murder Case. (It was by this time about nine in the morning – heir to quarter of a million sterling) and find:

▶ words which describe the area of Soho

▶ words which describe the people who live there.

Set out your work as follows:

Description of Soho	Description of people who live there
Dismal quarter	Slatternly passengers

Share your findings with the rest of the class and amend your notes as appropriate.

Moving On

1 Now look at the language Stevenson uses to describe the weather as Utterson approaches Hyde's living quarters. Find terms to complete the spidergram below.

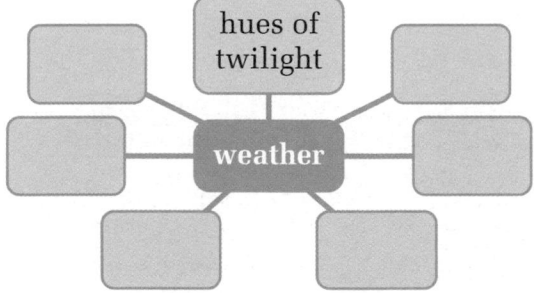

hues of twilight

weather

2 Find references to people living in this area. What kind of people are they?

3 Why do you think that Jekyll has chosen such an area to live as Hyde? What would be the advantages for him?

Share you answers with the rest of the class and amend your answers as appropriate.

Development

1 Look at the notes you have made on the two readings you have studied so far.

2 Use the information you have gathered to answer the following question:

In a novel where things are often hard to see clearly, why is Stevenson's use of setting and mood appropriate to the characters he puts into them?

Think about:

▶ The descriptions of London

▶ How the weather is used both to reveal and obscure sights and how this contributes to mood.

▶ The characters Stevenson places in these surroundings

▶ How the setting and mood are appropriate to the themes of:
secrecy;
reputation;
appearance versus reality.

You should write approximately 250 words.

Review

What have you learned about the way:

Stevenson uses an appropriate setting for the novel?

The way that the setting reinforces the idea of things being difficult to find out or to see?

Assignment Watch

In this Step you have looked at the way the gloomy, foggy and maze-like streets of London are a perfect setting for this novel of hidden truths and double lives.

Step 5 – Not My Fault!

In this Step you will explore an extract from Jekyll's suicide letter and consider the mixture of good and evil that Stevenson considers to be a part of every human being.

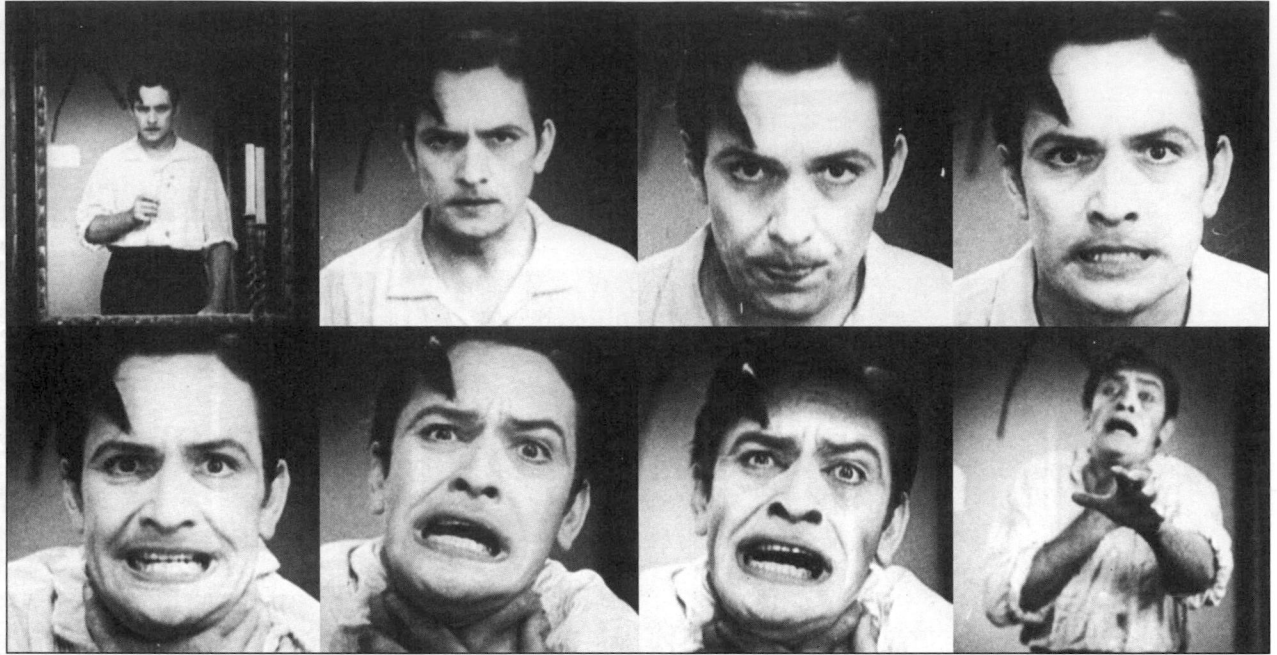

Frederic March transforming into Mr Hyde.

You Need to Know Box

Jekyll and Hyde are two sides of the same person. Hyde is seen as the more "primitive" of the two. He is the side of Jekyll that indulges his darkest thoughts without the slightest concern about the consequences for others. In this way, he is seen as man who has not fully evolved and is actually referred to as 'ape-like' on more than one occasion. He is an entirely selfish being who has difficulty in not physically assaulting those who stand in his way.

Hyde is the opposite of Jekyll in almost every way. Jekyll is a middle-aged, respectable, pleasant-looking, upstanding, professional member of the middle classes who is renowned for his good deeds. Hyde is a young, hairy, dwarfish man who has "something wrong with his appearance: something displeasing, something downright detestable".

The suggestion here is that criminality or sinfulness is a primitive condition. The upper and middle classes would consider themselves to be above such behaviour.

Starting Point

i) Write a definition of the word "conscience".

ii) Write down an example of a time when you were troubled by your conscience over something you did.

iii) Is it possible never to feel sorry or guilty for the bad things you have done?

Share your views with the rest of the class.

Moving On

Read the following section from Henry Jekyll's Full Statement of the Case below.

Men have before hired bravos to transact their crimes, while their own person and reputation sat under shelter. I was the first that ever did so for his pleasures. I was the first that could thus plod in the public eye with a load of genial respectability, and in a moment, like a schoolboy,
5 strip off these lendings and spring headlong into the sea of liberty. But for me, in my impenetrable mantle, the safety was complete. Think of it — I did not even exist! Let me but escape into my laboratory door, give me but a second or two to mix and swallow the draught that I had always standing ready; and whatever he had done, Edward Hyde would
10 pass away like the stain of breath upon a mirror; and there in his stead, quietly at home, trimming the midnight lamp in his study, a man who could afford to laugh at suspicion, would be Henry Jekyll.

    The pleasures which I made haste to seek in my disguise were, as I have said, undignified; I would scarce use a harder term. But in the hands of
15 Edward Hyde, they soon began to turn toward the monstrous. When I would come back from these excursions, I was often plunged into a kind of wonder at my vicarious depravity. This familiar that I called out of my own soul, and sent forth alone to do his good pleasure, was a being inherently malign and villainous; his every act and thought
20 centred on self; drinking pleasure with bestial avidity from any degree of torture to another; relentless like a man of stone. Henry Jekyll stood at times aghast before the acts of Edward Hyde; but the situation was apart from ordinary laws, and relaxed the grasp of conscience. It was Hyde, after all, and Hyde alone, that was guilty. Jekyll was no worse; he
25 woke again to his good qualities seemingly unimpaired; he would even make haste, where it was possible, to undo the evil done by Hyde. And thus his conscience slumbered.

    Into the details of the infamy at which I thus connived (for even now I can scarce grant that I committed it) I have no design of entering; I
30 mean but to point out the warnings and the successive steps with which my chastisement approached. I met with one accident which, as it brought on no consequence, I shall no more than mention. An act of cruelty to a child aroused against me the anger of a passer-by, whom I recognised the other day in the person of your kinsman; the doctor and
35 the child's family joined him; there were moments when I feared for my life; and at last, in order to pacify their too just resentment, Edward Hyde had to bring them to the door, and pay them in a cheque drawn in the name of Henry Jekyll. But this danger was easily eliminated from the future, by opening an account at another bank in the name of
40 Edward Hyde himself; and when, by sloping my own hand backward, I had supplied my double with a signature, I thought I sat beyond the reach of fate.

bravos: hired killers

genial: cheerful

mantle: cloak

familiar: friend

bestial avidity: disgusting enthusiasm

infamy: horrible act

chastisement: punishment

The fact that *The Strange Case of Dr Jekyll and Mr Hyde* is presented as a "case" is important as Stevenson has done this to give it an air of "reality". The novel is presented as a collection of both legal and medical documents, and therefore the work of educated and respectable men.

It was during the Victorian period that what we would recognise as "Science" first acquired its authority. For the first time, people were recognised as professional scientists, rather than as gentlemen with an interest. It was also the time of the Industrial Revolution and many of the advances made in technology would have revolutionised the workplace and there was consequently a closer relationship between scientists and the government.

The Victorian age was also the time when science began to challenge some of the most deeply held beliefs about humans and their place in the universe. Perhaps the most famous example of this was Charles Darwin's *The Origin of Species* which claimed that human beings had evolved from apes.

As you can see, there are times in his statement, that Dr Jekyll goes to some pains to distance himself from Mr Hyde whilst at others, he seems to admit that they are one and the same person.

Answer the following questions and keep a record of your responses:

i) Look at the first paragraph. How does Henry Jekyll feel about his actions in this part of his confession? Find evidence to support your views.

ii) What effect does he suggest that Edward Hyde has on his character? Find evidence to support your views.

iii) How did Jekyll avoid being discovered when he trampled on the child?

iv) Look up the word "vicarious" in line 17. Is this an appropriate word for Jekyll to use?

Share your answers with the rest of the class.

Development

Find examples from the passage where:

▶ Jekyll admits his own guilt

▶ he considers that it is Hyde, a separate being, who is to blame for crimes committed.

You should look carefully at his use of "he" and "I".

The following table contains some examples to get you started. Copy the layout and examples and add more of your own.

Jekyll admitting his part in events	Jekyll claiming that Hyde is to blame
The pleasures which I made haste to seek in my disguise were, as I have said, undignified; I would scarce use a harder term.	… his every act and thought centred on self; drinking pleasure with bestial avidity from any degree of torture to another; relentless like a man of stone.

Share your ideas with the rest of the class.

Review

1 What have you learned about Henry Jekyll's conscience?

Think about:

the way Henry Jekyll thinks and feels
the way he feels about Edward Hyde.

2 How convincing is Jekyll's view of events?

3 What have you learned about human nature?

Assignment Watch

In this Step, you have explored Jekyll's dual personality: the mix of good and evil that Stevenson implies is part of human nature. You have also examined the way that Jekyll tries to soothe his own conscience and to preserve his own reputation by blaming Edward Hyde for taking control of his life.

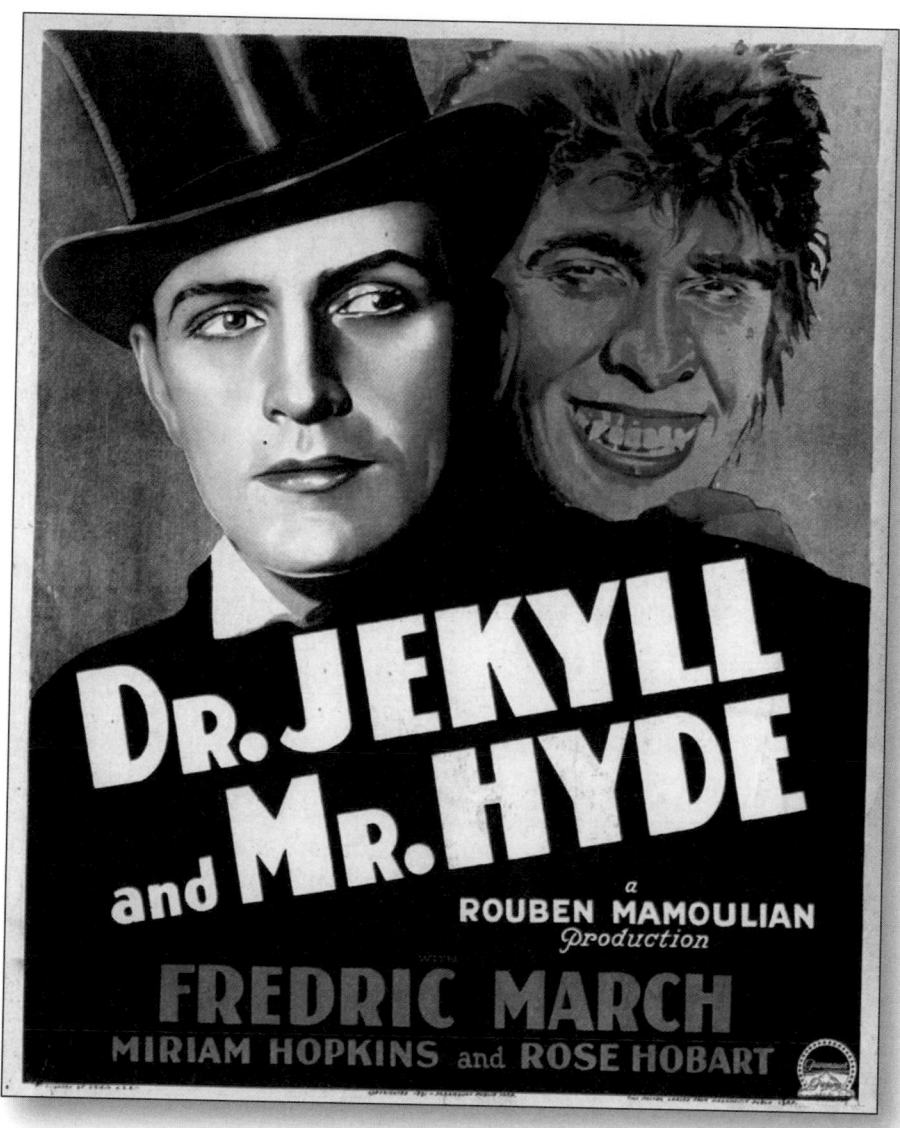

A poster from the 1931 film adaptation.

Step 5 – Tackling the Assignment

For your GCSE coursework folder, you will be asked to submit one of the following assignments.

Starting Point

Read the following and choose the assignment about which you feel most confident.

Assignment 1

1 "There are some things that are best kept private." To what extent does the opening chapter of *The Strange Case of Dr. Jekyll and Mr. Hyde* illustrate this view?

Assignment 2

2 What view of human nature does Stevenson present in the novel, *The Strange Case of Dr. Jekyll and Mr. Hyde*?

Assignment 3

3 In what way is *The Strange Case of Dr. Jekyll and Mr. Hyde* a novel of secrets, where the truth is hard to see?

Moving On

Read the section of the following flow chart which relates to your chosen assignment. Use it to help you to make a preliminary plan for your assignment.

Planning the assignment:		
Assignment	**Thinking:**	**Structure:**
1	For this question you should : ▶ think about what Utterson and Enfield reveal about themselves and what they keep to themselves ▶ consider what people like Utterson and Enfield think about privacy and a person's reputation ▶ how Utterson presents himself as more serious than he really is ▶ the different reasons people have for covering up the incident with the child ▶ the reasons why Utterson and Enfield are reluctant to pry any further into the Hyde's connection with Jekyll and what this tells us about the importance of privacy and reputation in the novel.	Look again at any notes you made about this scene. In your response, make sure that you : ▶ explain the aims and purpose of your writing ▶ explain how Utterson and Enfield hold back certain facts from public knowledge ▶ comment on the way Hyde's behaviour is dealt with and why it is covered up ▶ comment on the attitude of the time towards privacy and a person's reputation ▶ Support your ideas and views with evidence from the text ▶ provide a summary of the extent to which the opening chapter is about privacy and reputation.

Planning the assignment:		
Assignment	**Thinking:**	**Structure:**
2	This is a more open-ended question. It requires you to consider what we mean by human nature. Then you must consider the way it is presented by Stevenson. You should think about: ▶ how Jekyll/Hyde is used to reflect the mixture of good and evil in people ▶ how characters such as Utterson and Enfield feel about the importance of a person's reputation and the need to maintain a certain degree of privacy ▶ how the minor characters such as the doctor, the police officer, Hyde's servant, sometimes demonstrate emotions such as self interest, hatred or jealousy etc. ▶ supporting your ideas and views with evidence from the text ▶ Stevenson's view of human nature. In your planning, you should note: ▶ examples of how Jekyll/Hyde represents inner conflict ▶ how wanting people to think well of us is a part of human nature. Find examples of how that causes individuals in the novel to behave in ways that conceal their true motives ▶ examples of how characteristics such as self interest, jealousy, vindictiveness and hatred are also part of human nature.	In your response, make sure that you : ▶ explain the aims and purpose of your writing ▶ describe Hyde's actions and explain what they tell us about human nature ▶ comment on the behaviour of Enfield and Utterson and reflect on what it says about human nature ▶ describe the minor characters' actions and thoughts and reveal what they tell us about human nature ▶ Support your ideas and views with evidence from the text ▶ Summarise and comment on Stevenson's views of human nature.
	Thinking:	**Structure:**
3	For this question, you need to think about: ▶ the importance the characters place upon their privacy ▶ what we are told about them and what we must guess ▶ suspicions that are raised but left unanswered e.g. what was Sir Danvers Carew doing by the river late at night? What was in his letter to Utterson? ▶ the way London is presented in the novel and why this is appropriate in terms of atmosphere and mood.	▶ explain the aims and purpose of your writing ▶ describe how characters are not always what they seem and how they have private, secret sides to their lives ▶ give examples of where the reader must play detective to guess at what has been going on ▶ explain why the setting is appropriate for a novel of double lives and shifting identities.

Development

You are now going to work with others who have chosen the same assignment.

Use your preliminary notes and the bullet points in the thinking section of the flow chart to help you to develop the plan for your assignment.

Review

Discuss the notes you have made with the rest of the class.

Talk about:

▶ the way that privacy and reputation are features of the novel

▶ what Stevenson has to say about human nature.

N.B.

Before you start to write your assignment, you should spend some time reading the Boost Your Grade on pages 103–106 that the examining board will use to assess your response and discuss them.

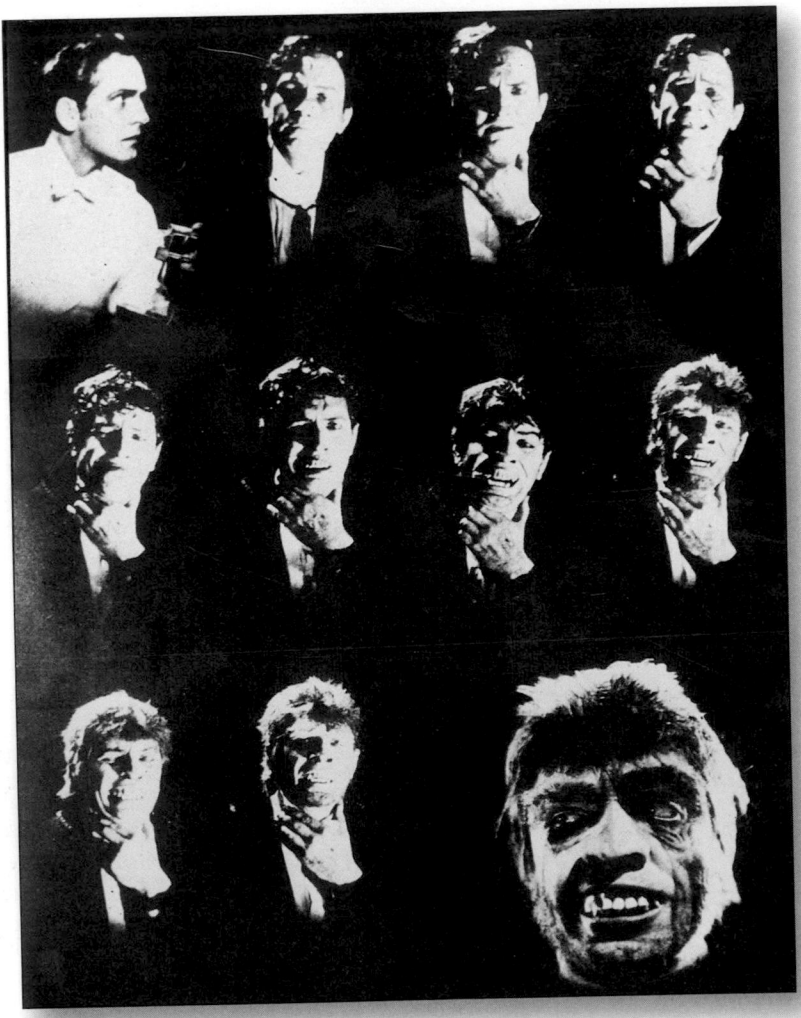

Stills from a film version from 1920.

Boost Your Grade

Starting Point

Before you start to write your assignment, you are going to examine what makes a successful response.

Listed below are the criteria that the examiner will use to assess your work. Read them carefully and use them to help you to assess the students' work that follows.

Prose Study	General Criteria	Specific Criteria
Grade E	Candidates make a personal response to texts, commenting on key ideas, themes and characters. They make inferences and deductions and identify some features of language and structure. They refer to aspects of the text when explaining their views.	Candidates show familiarity when describing: ▶ the purpose of a text ▶ characterisation, situation and narrative ▶ impact on readers.
Grade C	Candidates give a personal and critical response to literary texts that show understanding of the ways in which meaning is conveyed. They refer to aspects of language, structure and themes to support their views.	Candidates show analytical skill when exploring: ▶ implications, contemporary relevance and historical context of a text ▶ style, structure and characterisation ▶ language as characteristic of the writer and period.
Grade A	Candidates appreciate and analyse alternative interpretations, making cross-references where appropriate. They develop their ideas in full and refer in detail to aspects of language, structure and presentation, making apt and careful comparison within and between texts.	Candidates show analytical and interpretative skills when evaluating: ▶ the moral and philosophical context of a text ▶ significant achievements within prose fiction genre ▶ the writer's inventiveness with language for emotive, ironic or figurative effect.

Make a note of anything about the criteria you don't understand.

Discuss any concerns you have about the criteria with your teacher.

Moving On

On pages 104 and 105 are two extracts of students writing. The first is about the way Dickens' use of setting in *Great Expectations* helps to build sympathy for Pip. The second is about human nature in *The Strange Case of Dr Jekyll and Mr Hyde*. Each one is followed by the examiner's comments.

◀Excerpt 1▶

This excerpt was written in response to Assignment 2 for Great Expectations.

Another way in which Dickens makes me feel sympathy for Wemmick is through the setting of the chapter. Wemmick is an odd man but likeable and he is very proud of his home and his father who he calls 'The Aged'. The description of his house and garden show me that he is strange but harmless. Dickens starts by describing his cottage.

The top of it was cut out and painted like a battery mounted with guns.

"My own doing," said Wemmick. Looks pretty; don't it?"

He is very pleased by what he has done and wants to show it to Pip because he likes him. He does not seem to realise that it is in bad taste. I would probably feel sorry for him if he was embarrassed but he does not seem to notice.

I also like the way that he thinks that it is important that he can survive in his castle. From the setting, we learn that he keeps pigs, and rabbits and that he grows his own vegetables. He says:

"If you can suppose the little place besieged, it would hold out a devil of a time in point of provisions."

He means that he has so many animals and vegetables that he could live without the outside world for a long time. This shows he is proud of himself and likes being independent.

He also has part of his garden organised to look like an island with a pool and a fountain. This shows he has some imagination.

The final impression I have of Wemmick is that he is a good, kind man with very little taste but he does not realise it and so is proud of his work on his house. It would be hard not to like him.

Assessor's Comments

This candidate has made **some references to the setting** of the extract and suggested how it is used as a device to help build sympathy for Wemmick. There is evidence that the **character of Wemmick has been understood** as a likeable and harmless eccentric with very poor taste. However, it is equally clear that **some points are not fully developed** and that not all quotes are commented upon fully. Nevertheless, there is a clear attempt to respond to the issue of devices required in the question and there is a lively personal response to the extract. The writing is clear and spelling, punctuation and grammar are sound. Literature: Grade C; Reading (En2): Grade C

Though Grade C is available at both Foundation and Higher Tiers, work that is consistently of this standard would suggest that this student is likely to be entered for examination at the Higher Tier.

Excerpt 2

This excerpt was written in response to Assignment 2 for
The Strange Case of Dr Jekyll and Mr Hyde.

So, when we look at Stevensons' own views about good and bad in society, we begin to understand some of the conflict we see in the Jekyll/Hyde character. In the part of the story where we learn about Jekyll's statement we see that sometimes he seems very pleased with himself. He says that he did things as Hyde that other people might only think about doing or if they did want them to happen they would get "hired bravos" to do it for them. Yet when he thinks about how "malign and villainous" some of the things he did as Hyde were, he starts to see Hyde almost as someone else who was taking control and in that case, Hyde must take the blame for what happened. In other words it was nothing to do with the nice Dr. Jekyll, it was all nasty Mr. Hyde's fault.

In this way, Stevenson uses Jekyll/Hyde as a device to show that good versus evil is part of the inner man for all of us.

Assessor's Comment

In this part of the response, the candidate is beginning to explore the very complex idea at the heart of the question. There is a **clarity to the explanation,** which draws on some knowledge about **Stevensons's personal viewpoint** and links that with the Jekyll/Hyde personality. S/he begins to show understanding of the way in which the conflict is characterised.

There is **some relevant reference to text,** though at this point, it is limited.

The writing is well organised with sound spelling, punctuation and grammar. However, the statements/opinions expressed would need fuller development to move this response to the upper end of the grade range.

Literature Grade: C   En2 (Reading) Grade: C

1 Find evidence to support the examiner's comments.

2 Make notes for use in a class discussion.

Discuss your findings with your teacher.

Development

Below is the work of two more students writing about *Great Expectations*. They are both responding to Question 1 on page 78.

1 Read each extract.

2 Write a commentary, similar to the examiner's, in which you list the strengths and weaknesses of each extract. You should comment on the candidate's ability to:

▶ show an understanding of the characters

▶ explain *how* Dickens makes us feel sympathy for the characters

▶ refer closely to incidents in the text and use relevant quotation

▶ explain the effect that Dickens' use of language might have on the reader

3 Use the assessment criteria on page 103 to decide on an approximate grade for each piece of writing.

Extract 3

One of the other characters I feel sorry for is Miss Havisham. She was jilted on her wedding day and this has ruined her life forever. She has wilted and shrunk from a normal woman's size and is now pale and thin. Dickens uses lots of vocabulary to make her seem weak; words such as "corpse-like" and "shrunk to skin and bone". Also when Pip tells her he cannot play because the place is new and strange to him, she says,

"so new to him so old to me; so strange to him, so familiar to me; so melancholy to both of us!"

Dickens makes me feel sorry for her by describing the way she looks and by the words he gives her to say which create a sad life. Even though she is bad tempered and can be nasty, she is a sad person whose life is ruined.

Review

1 Share your thoughts with the rest of the class. How successful is each candidate? Make sure that you are able to justify why you have awarded the grade you have and ensure that you look at the criteria.

2 Summarise the key features of writing successfully about literary texts like *Great Expectations*.

Extract 4

I feel sorry for Pip when he meets Miss Havisham. He is only a young boy and he has to visit an old woman in a very strange house. The writer tells us how he feels. It is really sad at the end of the story when Estella makes him feel poor and not as important as her. He says he cried and kicked the wall and pulled his hair because he feels so bad about himself. Dickens makes him sound really hurt. I think it is a really good idea to tell the story through Pip because he is able to show us exactly how he feels.

Twentieth-Century Drama

Introduction

Objectives

In successfully completing this unit, you will:

▶ discuss and make notes on a character from a play you have read

▶ identify important themes and issues raised in the play

▶ understand the meaning of the term 'role'

▶ explore the social and historical context of the play

▶ consider the role of a major character in the play you are studying

▶ explore the staging of a key scene

▶ read short extracts from *An Inspector Calls* and *Blood Brothers*

▶ read extracts from responses to assignments based on the plays *An Inspector Calls* and *Blood Brothers*.

Plan and present your final piece of work for GCSE assessment.

If your chosen text is *An Inspector Calls*, you will follow the steps on pages 108 to 120. The steps for *Blood Brothers* are on pages 121 to 141. The assignments on page 142 apply to both texts.

GCSE

You will:

▶ complete a GCSE Literature coursework assignment

▶ develop the Reading skills you need for the GCSE examination

▶ complete a GCSE Speaking and Listening component in both group discussion and formal presentation.

Coursework and Examination Skills

▶ *Reading* – analytical reading of a drama text to show understanding and evaluation skills

▶ *Writing* – working co-operatively with others in a group presentation

▶ *Speaking and Listening* – working co-operatively with others in a group discussion.

It is expected that students will have already read the play and/or seen the film.

An Inspector Calls is more than a thriller written for the stage. On the one hand, it is written in the style of a 'whodunit', in which Inspector Goole shows how each of the characters is partially responsible for the death of Eva Smith (or Daisy Renton). However, it is also a play in which the writer is expressing his social and political views.

None of the characters is actually guilty of murder but each of them is 'inspected' by the Inspector and he exposes their faults. It is through this 'device' that JB Priestley questions the society of the time and the values it places on its people.

Starting Point

Your teacher will start by splitting the class into groups and allocating one character to each group. The characters are:

▶ Arthur Birling

▶ Sybil Birling

▶ Sheila Birling

▶ Eric Birling

▶ Gerald Croft

▶ Inspector Goole.

Use the example given opposite to help you make a spidergram to show the things you have learned about the character you have been allocated. Think about:

> physical descriptions
> likes/dislikes   marital status
> social class   personal history
> strengths/weaknesses.

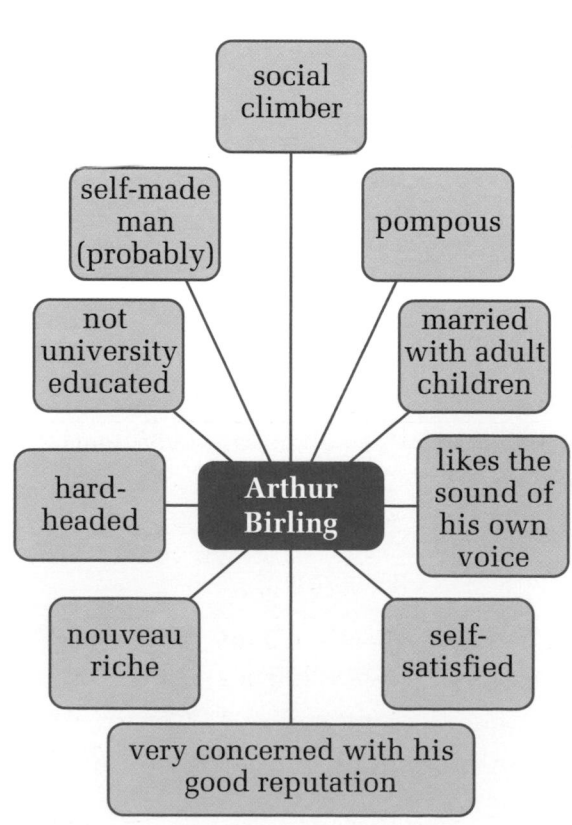

Key Concept

You may have found that several pieces of the information you have noted apply to the same aspect of a person's character, known as **personality**. For example, using words like 'warm', 'kind' or 'generous' would all describe someone's personality. Other words could combine to describe aspects such as social background, education, views and opinions, etc. These different aspects are known as **characteristics**.

Moving On

Now look for evidence from the text to support what you have said about your character. Find four lines from the play relating to the character and explain why you feel they are important in terms of letting us know about what sort of person he or she is.

When you have decided on which quotations to use, make a two-column table with the headings 'Characteristic' and 'Evidence'. For example:

Characteristic	Evidence
pompous and self-satisfied	"There's a good deal of silly talk about these days – but – and I speak as a hard-headed business man who has to take risks and know what he's about – I'say you can ignore all this silly pessimistic talk."
not university educated	"It's about time you learn't to face a few responsibilities. That's something this public school and varsity life you've had doesn't seem to teach you."
hard-headed business man	"Well, it's my duty to keep labour costs down, and if I'd agreed to this demand for a new rate we'd have added about twelve percent to our labour costs."

Development

Prepare notes for a three- to five-minute talk on your given character.

▸ List the points you wish to make.

▸ List the evidence that supports your views.

▸ Decide on the form of your presentation – you may wish to use OHTs, a flipchart, Powerpoint, lists, spidergrams, etc.

▸ Decide on the role of each person in your presentation.

Make your presentation to the class.

Review

What have you learned about the characters in the play? Think about:

▸ whether all the members of the Birling family hold the same views

▸ whether there is a difference between Sheila and Eric and their parents.

Assignment Watch

Your understanding of the characters and the roles that they play in the drama will be important when you come to evaluate the ideas that JB Priestley is presenting in this play.

Step 2 – Role

1 You Need to Know

Although *An Inspector Calls* was written in 1940, it is set in 1912, two years before the beginning of the First World War.

The war affected the economy very badly and, following a short boom after 1918, there was a slump which lasted throughout the 1930s. In 1926 there was what was called the General Strike, during which three million workers stopped work in response to an appeal from the Trade Union Congress.

In 1934, Priestley published a travel book entitled *English Journey*, in which he wrote about the enormous differences in the quality of life of the time. He described how areas that had been the base of nineteenth-century heavy industry, which had helped to make the nation a rich country, were now suffering and over-run by slum housing. He wrote: 'this England makes up the larger part of the Midlands and the North…but is not being added to and has no new life poured into it', and contrasted them with the more prosperous areas in the South.

Key Concept

The purpose(s) served by a character in a play is known as his or her **role**.

A writer may use characters for a range of purposes. For example, one character may fulfil the role of narrator; another may be used to reveal the author's feelings about certain kinds of people or issues; yet another may be used to keep the audience informed of some of the action not shown on stage.

Starting Point

Look up the words 'capitalism' and 'socialism' in a dictionary and write a definition for each one.

Share your definitions with the class to make sure that you understand what they mean.

One of the most recent productions (in the Garrick Theatre, London) used extras on stage to represent the working classes.

Moving On

1 Read the following speech by Birling in Act One near the beginning of the play, and answer the questions on p112.

Birling
　　Just let me finish, Eric. You've a lot to learn yet. And I'm talking as a hard-headed, practical man of business. And I say there isn't a chance of war. The world's developing so fast that it'll make war impossible. Look at the progress we're making. In a year or two we'll have aeroplanes that will be able to go anywhere.
　5　And look at the way the automobile's making headway – bigger and faster all the time. And then ships. Why, a friend of mine went over this new liner last week – the *Titanic* – she sails next week – forty-six thousand eight hundred tons – forty-six thousand eight hundred tons – New York in five days – and every luxury – and unsinkable, absolutely unsinkable. That's what you've got to keep your eye on,
　10　facts like that, progress like that – and not a few German officers talking nonsense and a few scaremongers here making a fuss about nothing. Now you three young people, just listen to this – and remember what I'm telling you now. In twenty or thirty years' time – let's say, in 1940 – you may be giving a little party like this – your son or daughter might be getting engaged – and I tell you by that
　15　time you'll be living in a world that'll have forgotten all these Capital versus Labour agitations and all these silly little war scares. There'll be peace and prosperity and rapid progress everywhere – except of course in Russia, which will always be behindhand, naturally.

Mr Birling making speeches.

2 Now answer these questions.

a) What do you think Birling's tone of voice is in this speech?

b) He refers to himself as a 'hard-headed, practical man of business'. What do you think he means by these words?

c) What do you think he means when he refers to 'all these Capital versus Labour agitations'? What does this tell you about the way he thinks of the threats from Trade Unions?

d) Can you say anything about his political opinions from this speech?

e) Birling makes several confident predictions for the future. Bearing in mind that the play is set in 1912, but was written in 1940, which of the predictions are wrong?

f) Why do you think Priestley has given Birling so many wrong predictions? What impression do you gain of Priestley's views about 'progress', as described by Birling? Give reasons for your answers.

g) Birling only thinks of progress in terms of advances in technology, improvements in goods and services and new ways of making money. How important do you think progress is in terms of the quality of people's lives? Think about living conditions, working conditions, pay, labour relations, etc.

h) Can you think of any examples where progress, as Birling sees it, might result in the lives of ordinary people being made worse? For example, think about working practices in factories; and new technology in the workplace and as used by the armed forces.

3 Now read the Inspector's parting speech on the following page and answer the questions:

Inspector
But just remember this. One Eva Smith has gone – but there are millions and millions and millions of Eva Smiths and John Smiths still left with us, with their lives, their hopes and fears, their suffering, and chance of happiness, all intertwined with our lives, with what we think and say and do. We don't live alone. We are members of one body. We are responsible for each other. And I tell you that the time will soon come when, if men will not learn that lesson, then they will be taught it in fire and blood and anguish. Good night.

a) What point do you think the Inspector is trying to make when he says that people like Eva Smith have 'hopes and fears that are intertwined with our lives'?

b) Birling would probably think of people such as Eva Smith in terms of wages and profit and loss sheets, and not as an individual human being with their own hopes and fears. What do you think would be the Inspector's opinion of this?

c) 'And I tell you that the time will come when if men will not learn that lesson, then they will be taught it in fire and blood and anguish'. What is the tone of these lines? What sort of event do you think the Inspector might be talking about when he says this?

Share your answers with the class.

Development

Using the notes you have made, answer one of the following in writing.

1 Birling and Goole are used by the playwright to represent two different political ideas. Explain:

▶ what you think each stands for

▶ where you think the playwright's sympathies lie.

Use quotations from the play to support what you say. You should write at least 100 words.

2 Now that you understand that characters in a play may be there to represent ideas, look at the other characters in the play. Concentrate on how (and if) they change over the course of the action.

▶ What is their role in the play?

▶ Where do they stand in relation to the Inspector and Birling?

▶ Have they learned anything as the play progresses? Do they hold essentially the same views at the end as at the beginning?

Review

What have you learned about how characters may be used to represent particular views and opinions of the author? Think about:

▶ what you understand by the idea of role in drama

▶ what you think Inspector Goole represents. Is he a realistic character or has he been created by the playwright to question the values held by the Birling family?

Niall Buggy as the Inspector and Diane Fletcher as Mrs Birling, Playhouse Theatre, London 2001.

Assignment Watch

The characters and their social backgrounds and beliefs are of great importance in *An Inspector Calls*. Understanding this will be very useful if you are to comment on the characters and their roles in the drama.

You Need to Know

As stated in the first Step, the play combines several dramatic forms. These include the morality play, the detective story (or whodunit) and naturalistic drama.

The **morality play** is a dramatised allegory (nearly always religious in nature) in which virtues, vices, diseases and temptations appear as characters who try to lead the hero astray as he makes his way in the world. From watching these plays, the audience would have been able to derive a simple Christian message in terms of the right and wrong way to lead their lives. They were popular in the fifteenth and sixteenth centuries.

The **detective story** is where a crime (usually murder) is committed by one of a group of people. The culprit will then be discovered by a detective who uncovers clues and unravels the mystery through a process of deduction and elimination.

Naturalistic drama is where the playwright attempts to give a very detailed depiction of 'real life' on the stage, especially with regard to speech, costume and sets. Furthermore, naturalistic drama often provides detailed and fully researched investigations into unexpected corners of society.

Starting Point

Read the You Need to Know box on this page and discuss the questions below.

1 Why do you think J.B. Priestley has chosen these three forms? In what way are they appropriate for the play's content?

2 How easy is it for a playwright to comment on the whole of society by focusing on just one family? How successful do you think Priestley is at showing the audience the social conditions at the time?

3 Apart from Eva Smith, there are several characters who are mentioned briefly in the play but never make an appearance. Read the short extracts opposite and on p115 and answer the following:

▶ What impressions do you get of Lady Croft, Alderman Meggarty and Charlie Brunswick? What can you say about them?

▶ What does it tell you about the "respectable" society in which the Birlings live?

Birling
    I have an idea that you mother – Lady Croft – while she doesn't object to my girl feels that you might have done better for yourself socially –

GERALD, rather embarrassed, begins to murmur some dissent, but BIRLING checks him.

    No Gerald, that's all right. Don't blame her. She comes from an old country family – landed people and so forth – and it's only natural.

Gerald
    She looked young and fresh and charming and altogether out of place there. And obviously she wasn't enjoying herself. Old Joe Meggarty, half-drunk and goggle-eyed had wedged her into a corner with that fat obscene carcass of his –
Mrs B
    There's no need to be disgusting and surely you don't mean Alderman Meggarty?

Gerald

It happened that a friend of mine, Charlie Brunswick, had gone off to Canada for six months and had let me have the key of a nice little set of rooms he had in – in Morgan Terrace – and had asked me to keep an eye on them for him and use them if I wanted to.

Moving On

1 Look at how each act ends. To what extent does each end on a cliffhanger?

2 Why do you think that Priestley chose to split the play into three acts? Consider that each new act begins precisely after the previous act finishes.

Act One

The Birling Family, Gerald and the Inspector are introduced. We hear why Mr Birling fired Eva/Daisy, how Sheila had her fired from a second job and Gerald's private admission to his fiancée of his relationship with her. Eric leaves.

Act Two

Gerald tells the story of his affair with the girl and Mrs Birling explains how she refused her charity when she was pregnant. Eric returns.

Act Three

Eric admits his involvement with the girl – that he got her pregnant and stole to support her. The final act deals with the characters reactions to their guilt and apparent hoax before the final phone call brings the play back to the beginning.

Share your thoughts with the rest of the class.

Development

1 Look at how the characters react to finding out that Inspector Goole is not a real police inspector. How does this affect the way they see things? Consider the way in which each of the characters thinks about this fact.

2 How do the different characters' reactions provide a dramatic ending to the play? Why is this effective? Think about the telephone call at the end of the play.

3 At the end of the play, there is no closure. We learn that each of the characters has had a part to play in Eva Smith's suicide, and the audience is invited to survey the overall scene – the chain of events that have led to the outcome, which was revealed at the beginning of the play. Is this appropriate?

4 Do you think it fitting that the story seems to start all over again at the end? Explain your answer.

5 How do you think the characters will respond to the second Inspector's questions? Will they respond in the same way, or will there be marked changes?

Review

What have you learned about the way structure and form can contribute towards:

▷ the way the audience reacts to the play?

▷ the overall meaning of the play?

Assignment Watch

When you come to assess the roles of the characters, it will help to have an understanding of the writer's intentions, how suspense is built up and how the action of the play fits together.

Step 4 – *Staging Issues*

In this part of the unit, you will be working on an important scene from the play. In particular, you will be thinking about how it might be staged in a production.

A 1995 production at The Garrick Theatre, London.

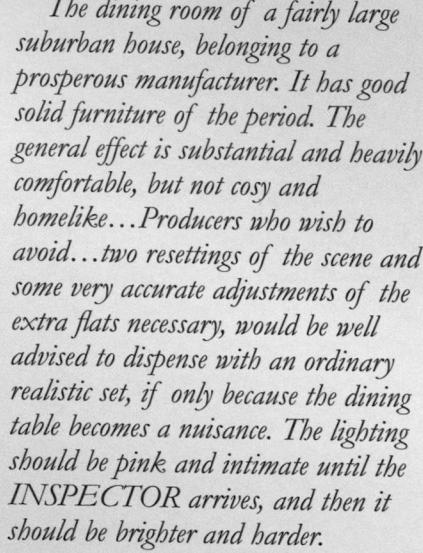

The dining room of a fairly large suburban house, belonging to a prosperous manufacturer. It has good solid furniture of the period. The general effect is substantial and heavily comfortable, but not cosy and homelike...Producers who wish to avoid...two resettings of the scene and some very accurate adjustments of the extra flats necessary, would be well advised to dispense with an ordinary realistic set, if only because the dining table becomes a nuisance. The lighting should be pink and intimate until the INSPECTOR arrives, and then it should be brighter and harder.

Starting Point

List the things that a director has to think about when he or she is preparing a drama text for production. For example, he or she will need to think about characters' movement on stage and gestures.
What else needs to be considered?
Try to come up with at least five points.

Share your thoughts with the rest of the class.

Now have a look at the stage directions at the beginning of the play.

1 What do you think Priestley means by the phrases 'substantial and heavily comfortable' and 'not cosy and homelike'?

2 What do these things tell us about the Birlings and their home?

3 How might a director arrange the set to recreate the effect that Priestley is looking for?

Share your thoughts with the rest of the class.

Moving On

You are now going to read an extract from early in the play, at the point where the Inspector arrives at the Birling house. You will then discuss the how this scene could be staged.

1 Read the extract below.

Birling [*solemnly*]
   But this is point. I don't want to lecture you two young fellows again. But what so many of you don't seem to understand now, when things are so much easier, is that a man has to make his own way – has to look after himself – and his family too, of course, when he has one – and so long as he does that he won't come to much harm. But the way some of these cranks talk and write now, you'd think
5   that everyone has to look after everyone else, as if we were all mixed up together like bees in a hive – community and all that nonsense. But take my word for it, you youngsters – and I've learned in the good hard school of experience – that a man has to mind his own business and look after himself and his own – and –

   [*We hear the sharp ring of the front door bell. Birling stops to listen.*]

Eric
10   Somebody at the front door.
Birling
   Edna'll answer it. Well, have another glass of port, Gerald – and then we'll join the ladies. That'll stop me giving you good advice.
Eric
   Yes, you've piled it on a bit tonight Father.
Birling
   Special occasion. And feeling contented, for once, I wanted you to have the
15   benefit of my experience.

   [*EDNA enters.*]

Edna
   Please, sir, an inspector's called.
Birling
   An inspector? What kind of inspector?
Edna
   A police inspector. He says his name's Inspector Goole.
Birling
   Don't know him. Does he want to see me?
Edna
20   Yes, sir. He says it's important.
Birling
   All right, Edna. Show him in here. Give us some more light.

   [*EDNA does, then goes out.*]

   I'm still on the Bench. It may be something about a warrant.

Gerald [lightly]

Sure to be. Unless Eric's been up to something. [Nodding confidentially to Birling] And that would be awkward, wouldn't it?

Birling [humorously]

25   Very.

Eric [who is uneasy, sharply]

Here, what do you mean?

Birling [lightly]

Only something we were talking about when you were out. A joke really.

Eric [still uneasy]

Well, I don't think it's very funny.

Birling [sharply, staring at him]

What's the matter with you?

Eric [defiantly]

30   Nothing.

Edna [opening door, and announcing]

Inspector Goole.

[The INSPECTOR enters, and Edna goes, closing the door after her.
The INSPECTOR need not be a big man but he creates at once an impression of massiveness, solidity and purposefulness. He is a man in his fifties, dressed in a plain darkish suit of the period. He speaks carefully, weightily, and has a disconcerting habit of looking hard at the person he addresses before actually speaking.]

Inspector

Mr Birling?

Birling

Yes. Sit down, Inspector.

Inspector [sitting]

Thank you, sir.

Birling

35   Have a glass of port – or a little whisky?

Inspector

No, thank you Mr Birling. I'm on duty.

Birling

You're new aren't you?

Inspector

Yes sir. Only recently transferred.

Birling

I thought you must be. I was an alderman for years – and Lord Mayor two years
40   ago – and I'm still on the Bench – so I know the Brumley police officers pretty well – and I thought I'd never seen you before.

Inspector

Quite so.

Birling

Well, what can I do for you? Some trouble about a warrant?

Inspector

No, Mr Birling.

Birling [after a brief pause, with a touch of impatience]
45   Well, what is it then?
Inspector
        I'd like some information, if you don't mind, Mr Birling. Two hours ago, a young
        woman died in the Infirmary. She'd been taken there this afternoon because she'd
        swallowed a lot of strong disinfectant. Burned her insides out, of course.
Eric: [involuntarily]
        My God!
Inspector
50   Yes, she was in great agony. They did everything they could for her at the
        Infirmary, but she died. Suicide of course.
Birling [rather impatiently]
        Yes, yes. Horrible business. But I don't understand why you should come here,
        Inspector –
Inspector [cutting through, massively]
        I've been around to the room she had, and she'd left a letter and a sort of diary.
55   Like a lot of these young women who get into various kinds of trouble, she'd used
        more than one name. But her original name – her real name – was Eva Smith.

2 Before you decide on how you would stage
the scene. Consider the following questions.

a) How will Birling deliver the speech at
the opening to the extract? Consider
what kind of man he is and how he
might deliver his words.

b) What Birling is saying sums up his
views on politics and society. Is it
important that the Inspector's arrival
cuts off this speech? Would you
emphasise this on stage? How?

c) Look at the words Edna uses when she
speaks to Birling. What do they suggest
about the kind of a relationship she has
with the family? How would you want
to represent her character on stage?
Think about gestures, attitude, facial
expression, etc.

d) Why might Eric not find 'the joke' very
funny? How would you show his
nervousness?

e) According to the stage directions, the
Inspector need not be a big man, but he
must convey "massiveness, solidity and
purposefulness". What exactly do you
think Priestley means by this and how
will you show it on stage?

f) The lights are turned up when the
Inspector is shown in (as requested by
Birling and mentioned in the opening
stage instructions). Why is this
appropriate? What effect will it have on
how the audience see and think about
the characters on the stage?

g) The Inspector cuts off Birling in the
middle of his speech. Do you think
Birling used to people interrupting
what he says? How do you think he
will react to this?

Development

1 Now discuss how you will present the scene. Bearing in mind your responses to the questions you have just answered, you should:

(i) consider how you will interpret the author's directions for the stage set

(ii) think about appearance of the characters. Will Birling, Eric, and Gerald be dressed identically or might there be slight differences?

(iii) consider the role of the characters in the scene and how you would bring this out on stage. Refer to the work you did in Step 2.

(iv) identify any particularly important lines and decide how they should be spoken

(v) interpret the stage directions given by the author and decide if or how you will follow them

(vi) decide on the tone, type of voice, accent and gestures that the characters should use

(vii) determine any sound effects, special effects, extra props or music you would use. You must be able to explain why you have included these things (if you choose to do so) and how they add to your interpretation.

2 Summarise your thoughts for each of the above into a series of bullet points and be ready to report them to the class. Be sure that you can discuss the reasons for your staging decisions and interpretation of the characters.

Present your views to the rest of the class.

Review

Share your thoughts with the rest of the class. What have you learned about the key issues a director must consider in staging a play?

Assignment Watch

In your answers to the assignment questions, it is important that you respond to the play as a piece of drama, as well as a written text. The ability to understand and interpret Priestley's dramatic methods and how they contribute to the meaning of the play is important.

A 1954 film version interpreted the scene like this.

Step 1 – Blood Brothers

This unit assumes that you will already have read the play *Blood Brothers* by Willy Russell. It contains several major characters, one of whom is Mrs Johnstone. She is a single mother, struggling to raise a large family in a poor neighbourhood in Liverpool. She is forced to take low-paid work as a cleaner for Mrs Lyons in order to survive. She has seven children and is pregnant with twins at the opening of the play. Mrs Johnstone agrees to give one of her newborn children to her employer, and so Eddie and Mickey, born to the same woman on the same day, embark on very different lives. The play shows the importance that a person's upbringing can have on the way their life develops.

Willy Russell uses the musical *Blood Brothers* to express his views about society at the end of the twentieth century. Although it certainly sets out to entertain, it also has much to say about life in Liverpool in the sixties and seventies. It not only dwells on the importance of the environment in which a person is raised, but also on the way in which society as a whole regards single mothers, in particular. In it, the playwright is putting forward his views about these and other issues.

In this step, you are going to examine the character of Mrs Johnstone.

Lyn Paul as Mrs Johnstone, Phoenix Theatre, London, 1998.

Starting Point

1 Look at this list of words and find at least eight that best describe Mrs Johnstone.

cruel   wealthy   loving   bitter

clever   poor   gullible   superstitious   angry   helpless

resourceful   liar   easy-going   rejected   devoted   self-centred

heartless   brave   happy   kind   struggling

determined   carefree

2 Now add three more words of your own to describe Mrs Johnstone.

3 Find some examples and/or quotes from the play that support your views. Set out your work in a table as follows:

Describing word	Evidence

Share your views with the rest of the class. Agree on a class list.

Moving On

At the beginning of the play, the narrator tells us that Mrs Johnstone has 'a stone' in the place of her heart. After all, she gives her son away to Mrs Lyons. The implications of the narrator's words are that a good mother would not do such a thing. Mrs Johnstone, therefore, must be hard, cruel and unfeeling. The events of the drama, however, allow the audience to judge the truth of this statement.

Before you can judge the quality of Mrs Johnstone as a mother, it is important to think about the qualities that we all look for in mothers.

List at least five things that you would expect of a 'good' mother. For example:

◗ a caring personality

◗ someone to share problems with.

Share your views with the rest of the class and form a class list of characteristics of a good mother.

Development

1 Look at the criteria that you have listed and discuss whether you feel that Mrs Johnstone demonstrates any of them. Is she a good mother?

2 Keep a record of your discussion that includes reasons for your views.

Share your thoughts with the rest of the class.

Review

What have you learned about:

◗ Mrs Johnstone's character?

◗ Mrs Johnstone as a mother?

Assignment Watch

Your understanding of the characters and the roles that they play in the drama will be important when you come to discuss the social and historical context of the play and evaluate the ideas that Willy Russell is putting forward.

Step 2 – Mrs Lyons – The Other Mother

You have already looked at the character of Mrs Johnstone and the kind of mother she is. She is one of the major female characters in the play. Another is Mrs Lyons, who 'adopts' Edward as a child. In this Step, you are going to consider Mrs Lyons as a character and compare her with Mrs Johnstone.

Starting Point

Use the following prompts to make notes on Mrs Lyons' character and lifestyle.

▶ How does Mrs Lyons spend her days before she takes Edward?

▶ Is she satisfied with her life? Give reasons.

▶ How does she treat Edward?

▶ Why does she sack Mrs Johnstone? Is she justified in doing so?

▶ What causes her to think that she is being pursued by Mrs Johnstone?

▶ How do you feel about her at the beginning of the play? Give reasons.

▶ Do your views change during the course of the play? Give reasons.

▶ Does Mrs Lyons deserve our sympathy or is she a villain? Explain your views carefully.

1 Share your thoughts with the rest of the class.

2 Update your notes.

Moving On

One of the great ironies in the play is that whilst Mrs Johnstone wishes she had some more money to help her to raise her family, Mrs Lyons, for all her possessions, is envious of Mrs Johnstone. Look at the song *My Child* that is printed on page 124.

1 What would having a child provide Mrs Lyons with?

2 What does Mrs Johnstone think that Mrs Lyons could provide for her child that she never could?

Share your thoughts with the rest of the class.

Development

You are now going to compare Mrs Johnstone and Mrs Lyons, as mothers. You will need to remind yourself of the criteria for being a good mother that you decided upon in the last Step, and also what you said about Mrs Johnstone.

1 Look at your criteria for a good mother to judge whether Mrs Lyons meets any of them. Make notes of your discussions.

2 What are the strengths and weaknesses of each character as a mother?

3 Is either of them a 'good' mother? Give reasons.

4 Do you sympathise with either of them?In this Step, you are going to look

MRS LYONS (singing): Each day I look out
from this window,
I see him with his friends, I hear him call,
I rush down as I fold my arms around him,
He's gone. Was he ever there at all?
I've dreamed of all the places I would
take him,
The games we'd play the stories I
would tell,
The jokes we'd share, the clothing I would
make him,
I reach out. But as I do. He fades away.

*The melody shifts into that of MRS
JOHNSTONE who is looking up at MRS
LYONS, feeling for her. MRS LYONS gives a
half smile and a shrug, perhaps slightly
embarrassed at what she has revealed. MRS
JOHNSTONE turns and looks at the room she
is in. Looking up in awe at the comparative
opulence and ease of the place. Tentatively and
wondering she sings*

MRS JOHNSTONE: If my child
was raised
In a palace like this one,
(He) wouldn't have to worry where
His next meal was comin' from.
His clothing would be (supplied by)
George Henry Lee.

*MRS LYONS sees that MRS JOHNSTONE
might be persuaded.*

MRS LYONS (singing): He'd have all his
own toys
And a garden to play in.
MRS JOHNSTONE: He could make too
much noise
Without the neighbours complainin'.
MRS LYONS: Silver trays to take meals on
MRS JOHNSTONE: A bike with both
wheels on?

MRS LYONS nods enthusiastically.

MRS LYONS And he'd sleep every night
In a bed of his own.

MRS JOHNSTONE: He wouldn't get into
fights
He'd leave matches alone
And you'd never find him
Effin' and blindin'.
And when he grew up
He could never be told
To stand and queue up
For hours on end at the dole
He'd grow up to be
MRS LYONS/MRS JOHNSTONE
(*together*): A credit to me.
MRS JOHNSTONE: To you.
MRS JOHNSTONE: I would still be able
to see him every day,
Wouldn't I?
MRS LYONS: Of course.
MRS JOHNSTONE: An'…an' you would
look after him,
wouldn't y'?
MRS LYONS (*singing*): I'd keep him warm
in the winter
And cool when it shines.
I'd pull out his splinters
Without making him cry.
I'd always be there
If his dream was a nightmare.
My child.
My child.

Review

What have you learned about:

▷ Mrs Lyons' character and lifestyle?

▷ why she wants to 'adopt' Edward
and the kind of mother she is?

Assignment Watch

Your understanding of Mrs Lyons
and the part she plays in the drama
will be important when you come to
discuss the social and historical
context of the play.

Step 3 – Role

In this Step, you are going to look at the way in which the Johnstone and the Lyons families are used by the author to represent the working classes and middle classes in Liverpool.

Key Concept

The purpose(s) served by a character in a play is known as his or her **role**.

A writer may use characters for a range of purposes. For example, one character may fulfil the role of narrator; another may be used to reveal the author's feelings about certain kinds of people or issues; yet another may be used to keep the audience informed of some of the action not shown on stage.

A lack of money is at the heart of both Mrs Johnstone and Mickey's problems in the play.

You Need to Know

Blood Brothers is set in sixties and seventies Liverpool. It reflects the period clearly with a poor working class and a wealthier middle class living side by side in the Liverpool suburbs.

The Johnstone family is working class. Mrs Johnstone has rushed into an early marriage due to pregnancy. She is poorly educated and rather superstitious. Her house is a rented terraced home situated in a poor neighbourhood that she struggles to pay for. Conditions are basic and cramped. She rewards her children from catalogues that offer her clothes and toys on the 'never, never', or hire purchase agreements, that means she can pay for her goods weekly. If she fails to make the regular payments, which happens frequently, the goods are repossessed. In the play Mrs Johnstone is resigned to the fact that she cannot always afford what she wants and that she will occasionally be visited by the bailiffs.

This is the only way she is able to provide her children with the things she wants for them. Mrs Johnstone's limited education means that the work she can do is restricted to poorly-paid jobs and so her horizons are limited. She is delighted when she is re-housed in Skelmersdale in a newly-built council house. Many of the slum houses in Liverpool and other big cities were demolished at this time and 'new towns' made up of council houses were built to replace them. Mrs Johnstone remarks in the song 'Moving House' that she will have a home with a parlour fit for the Pope to visit. She seems touchingly unaware that her new home is low budget and basic. Her upbringing has shaped her own horizons to the point that she is overjoyed about her new home.

By contrast, Mrs Lyons belongs to the wealthier middle class. She is a housewife with no need to work since her husband can provide comfortably for the family. She lives in a large house, can afford a cleaner and has the time to enjoy a leisurely lifestyle. Their aspirations are wide-ranging. Children brought up in this setting are surrounded by books, expected to succeed in life and may attend a public school. They would be expected to 'marry well' and to take up a prestigious and well-paid job.

Starting Point

Using the reading material on p125 and any ideas of your own, make two lists of words you associate with the terms 'working class' and 'middle class'. The following prompts may help you to build up a profile of each:

▶ type of housing

▶ job

▶ first names

▶ accent or way of speaking

▶ style of dress

▶ type of social life

▶ education

▶ ambitions.

Share your thoughts with the rest of the class.

Moving On

In the following scene, Mickey and Edward, both aged seven, meet for the first time. Edward has strayed from his own neighbourhood and has found Mickey, who has been playing with the boys and girls from his street.

1 Read the scene and answer the questions on page 129.

MICKEY *(suspiciously):* Hello.
EDWARD: I've seen you before.
MICKEY: Where?
EDWARD: You were playing with the boys near my house.
5 MICKEY: Do you live up near the park?
EDWARD: Yes. Are you going to come and play up there again?
MICKEY: No. I would do but I'm not allowed.
EDWARD: Why?
MICKEY: 'Cos me mam says.
10 EDWARD: Well, my mummy doesn't allow me to play down here actually.
MICKEY: 'Gis a sweet.
EDWARD: All right *(He offers a bag from his pocket.)*
MICKEY *(shocked):* What?
EDWARD: Here.
15 MICKEY *(trying to work out the catch. Suspiciously taking one):* Can I have another one
    for our Sammy?
EDWARD: Yes, of course. Take as many as you want.
MICKEY *(taking a handful)* Are you soft?
EDWARD: I don't think so.
20 MICKEY: Round here if y'ask for a sweet, y'have to ask about twenty million
    times. An 'y' know what?
EDWARD: *(sitting beside Mickey):* What?
MICKEY: They still don't bleedin' give y' one. Sometimes our Sammy does but
    y'have to be dead careful if out Sammy gives y' a sweet.
25 EDWARD: Why?
MICKEY: Cos if our Sammy gives y'a sweet he's usually weed on it first.

EDWARD *(exploding in giggles):* Oh, that sounds like super fun.
MICKEY: It is. If y' our Sammy.
EDWARD: Do you want to come and play?
30 MICKEY: I might do. But I'm not playin' now 'cos I'm pissed off.
EDWARD *(awed):* Pissed off. You say smashing things don't you? You know any
        more words like that?
MICKEY: Yeh. Yeh, I know loads of words like that. Y'know, like the 'F' word.
EDWARD *(clueless)* Pardon?
35 MICKEY: The 'F' word.

EDWARD is still puzzled. MICKEY looks round to check that he cannot be overheard, then
whispers the word to EDWARD. The two of them immediately wriggle and giggle with glee.

EDWARD: What does it mean?
MICKEY: I don't know. It sounds good though doesn't it?
EDWARD: Fantastic. When I get home, I'll look it up in the dictionary.
MICKEY: In the what?
40 EDWARD: The dictionary. Don't you know what a dictionary is?
MICKEY: 'Course I do… it's a, it's a thingy innit?
EDWARD: A book which explains the meaning of words.
MICKEY: The meaning of words, yeh. Our Sammy'll be here soon. I hope he's
        in a good mood. He's dead mean sometimes.
45 EDWARD: Why?
MICKEY: It's 'cos he's got a plate in his head.
EDWARD: A plate. In his head?
MICKEY: Yeh. When he was little, me Mam was at work an' our Donna Marie
        was supposed to be lookin' after him but he fell out the window an' broke
50   his head. So they took him to hospital an' put a plate in his head.
EDWARD: A plate. A dinner plate?
MICKEY: I don't think so, 'cos our Sammy's head's not really that big. It must
        have been one of those little plates that you have bread off.
EDWARD: A side plate?
55 MICKEY: No, it's on the top.
EDWARD: And…and can you see the shape of it, in his head?
MICKEY: I suppose, I suppose if y' looked under his hair.
EDWARD *(after a reflective pause):* You know the most smashing things. Will you
        be my best friend?
60 MICKEY: Yeh. If y' want.
EDWARD: What's your name?
MICKEY: Michael Johnstone. But everyone calls me Mickey. What's yours?
EDWARD: Edward Lyons.
MICKEY: Do they call y' Eddie?
65 EDWARD: No.
MICKEY: Well, I will.
EDWARD: Will you?
MICKEY: Yeh. How old are y' Eddie?
EDWARD: Seven.
70 MICKEY: I'm older than you. I'm nearly eight.
EDWARD: well, I'm nearly eight really.
MICKEY: What's your birthday?
EDWARD: July the eighteenth.
MICKEY: So is mine.

75   EDWARD: Is it really?

MICKEY: Ey. We were born on the same day… that means we can be blood brothers. Do you wanna be my blood brother, Eddie?

EDWARD: Yes, please.

MICKEY *(producing a penknife)* It hurts y'know. *(He puts a nick in his hand.)*
80   Now, give us yours.

MICKEY nicks EDWARD's hand, then they clamp hands together.

See this means that we're blood brothers, an' that we always have to stand by each other. Now you say after me: 'I will always defend my brother'.

EDWARD: I will always defend my brother…

MICKEY: And stand by him.

85   EDWARD: And stand by him.

MICKEY: An' share sweets with him.

EDWARD: And share…

Sammy leaps in front of them, gun in hand, pointed at them.

MICKEY: Hi ya, Sammy.

SAMMY: Give us a sweet.

90   MICKEY: Haven't got any…

EDWARD: Yes, you have…

MICKEY frantically shakes his head, trying to shut EDWARD up.

Yes, I gave you one for Sammy remember?

Sammy laughs at EDWARD's voice and MICKEY's misfortune.

SAMMY: Y' little robbin' get.

MICKEY: No, I'm not. *(He hands over a sweet.)* An' anyway, you pinched my best gun.

95   MICKEY tries to snatch the gun from Sammy, but Sammy is too fast.

SAMMY: It's last anyway. It only fires caps. I'm gonna get a real gun soon, I'm gonna get an air gun.

SAMMY goes into a fantasy shoot out. He doesn't notice EDWARD who has approached him and is trying to get a closer look at his head.

(Eventually noticing) What are you lookin' at?

EDWARD: Pardon.

100 MICKEY: That's Eddie. He lives up by the park.

SAMMY: He's a frggin' poshy.

MICKEY: No, he's not. He's my best friend.

SAMMY *(snorting, deciding it's not worth the bother)*: You're soft. Y' just soft little kids. *(In quiet disdain he moves away.)*

105 MICKEY: Where y' goin'?

SAMMY *(looking at MICKEY)*: I'm gonna do another burial. Me worms have died again.

MICKEY *(excitedly; to EDWARD)*: Oh, y' comin' the funeral? Our Sammy is having a Funeral. Can we come Sammy?

110 SAMMY puts his hand in his pocket and brings forth a handful of soil.

SAMMY: Look, they was alive an wrigglin' this mornin'. But by dinner time they was dead.

MICKEY and EDWARD inspect the deceased worms in Sammy's hand.

Con O'Neill and
Robert Locke as
Mickey and Edward,
Albery Theatre,
London, 1988.

a) What do the two boys Mickey and
Edward have in common?

b) How are they different? Give examples.

c) How might a director use costume to
bring out their differences?

d) Mickey and Edward are twins. Why are
there such differences between them?

2 Now read another scene from the play in
which Mickey and Edward are very much
older and answer the questions that follow.
Edward has returned from university and is
expecting to find Mickey in a party mood.
However, Mickey has had an eventful few
months: Linda is pregnant and he has
married her, and now he has been made
redundant from the factory where he
worked. He is feeling very depressed.

EDWARD enters in a duffle coat and college scarf, unseen by MICKEY.
EDWARD creeps up behind MICKEY and puts his hands over his eyes.

EDWARD: Guess who?
MICKEY: Father Christmas.
5   EDWARD *(leaping out in front of them):* Mickey… *(Laughing.)* Merry Christmas.
MICKEY, unamused, looks at EDWARD and then looks away. Come on then…I'm back,
     where's the action, the booze, the Christmas parties, the music and the birds?

No reaction.

     What's wrong Mickey?
MICKEY: Nothin'. How's University?
10 EDWARD: Mickey, it's fantastic. I haven't been to so many parties in my life.
     And there's so many tremendous people, but you'll meet them Mick, some
     of them, Baz, Ronnie and Clare and oh, lots of them. They're coming
     over for the New Year, for the party. Ooh it's just… it's great Mickey.
MICKEY: Good.
15 EDWARD: Come on, what's wrong? It's nearly Christmas, we were going to do
     everything. How's Linda?
MICKEY: She's OK.

EDWARD *(trying again to rally him)*: Well, come on then, let's go then… come on.
MICKEY: Come on where?
20   EDWARD: Mickey, what's wrong?
MICKEY: You. You're a dick head!

EDWARD is slightly unsure but laughs anyway.

There are no parties arranged. There is no booze or music. Christmas? I'm sick to the teeth of Christmas an' it isn't even here yet. See there's very little to celebrate, Eddie. Since you left I've been walking around all day, every
25   day, lookin' for a job.
EDWARD: What about the job you had?
MICKEY: It disappeared. *(Pause.)* Y' know somethin'. I bleedin' hated that job, standin' there all day never doin' nothin' but put cardboard boxes together. I used to get… I used to get terrified that I' have to do it for the rest of me
30   life. But after three months of nothin', the same answer everywhere, nothin' down for y', I'd crawl back to that job for half the pay and double the hours. Just makin' up boxes it was. But after bein' fucked off from everywhere, it seems like paradise.

Pause.

EDWARD : Why… why is a job so important? If I couldn't get a job I'd just say
35   sod it and draw the dole, live like a bohemian, tilt my hat to the world and say 'screw you'. So you're not working. Why is it so important?
MICKEY *(looking at him):* You don't understand anythin' do y'? I don't wear a hat that I could tilt at the world.
EDWARD: Look… come on… I've got money, plenty of it. I'm back, let's
40   forget about bloody jobs, let's go and get Linda and celebrate. Look, look, money, lots of it, have some…

(He tries to thrust some notes into MICKEY's hands.)

MICKEY: No, I don't want your money, stuff it.

He throws the notes to the ground. EDWARD picks them up and stands looking at MICKEY.

Eddie, just do me a favour an' piss off, will y'?

Pause.

EDWARD: I thought, I thought we always stuck together. I thought we were…
45   were blood brothers.
MICKEY: That was kid's stuff, Eddie. Didn't anyone tell y'? *(He looks at EDWARD.)* But I suppose you still are a kid, aren't y'?
EDWARD: I'm exactly the same age as you, Mickey.
MICKEY: Yeh. But you're still a kid. An I wish I could be as well Eddie, I wish I
50   could still believe in all that blood brother stuff. But I can't, because while no one was looking I grew up. An' you didn't, because you didn't need to; an I don't blame y' for it. Eddie. In your shoes I'd be the same, I'd still be able to be a kid. But, I'm not in your shoes, I'm in these, lookin' at you. An' you make me sick, right? That was all just kid's stuff Eddie, an 'I don't want
55   to be reminded of it. Right? So just take yourself away. Go an' see your friends and celebrate with them.

Pause.

Go on…beat it before I hit y'.

a) Why is having a job so important to Mickey?

b) Why is Mickey feeling so pressured by what has happened to him?

c) Edward fails to understand Mickey's situation. Why?

d) How might a director bring out the differences betwcen Edward and Mickey at this point in the play?

e) Why have their lives turned out so differently?

Share your answers with the class.

Development

Using the notes you have made, answer the following question in writing.

The playwright uses Mickey and Edward to represent two different social classes. Explain what you think character each stands for. You should write about 100 words.

Review

1 What do you understand by the idea of role in drama?

2 What have learned about:

▸ social class?

▸ the Johnstone and Lyons families?

▸ why are they different?

Assignment Watch

The characters and their social background are of great importance in *Blood Brothers*. Your understanding of this will be very useful if you are to comment on the characters and their roles in drama.

Con O'Neill and Mark Hutchinson as Edward and Mickey, Liverpool Playhouse, 1992.

Step 4 – The Play's Structure

Blood Brothers differs from many plays for a number of reasons. In this Step, you are going to look at two aspects of the play's structure and think about how they are used by Willy Russell to help to convey his views and ideas to the audience.

Blood Brothers is a musical, and when it was first produced in the West End of London one theatre critic said that the performance brought the audience "roaring to its feet" in approval of what they had seen. In particular, the music has played a big part in its success. However, whilst the music may be entertaining, we should also consider whether that is the only reason it is included. You are now going to look at what one of the songs adds to our understanding of the Johnstone family.

Starting Point

1 Read the song 'Bright New Day' and discuss:

▶ what Mrs Johnstone feels that the move will do for her family

▶ the effect the move has on Mrs Johnstone's morale

▶ how moving house will affect the people left behind in the neighbourhood

▶ whether a song is an appropriate way of conveying this information to the audience.

Give reasons for your answers.

MRS JOHNSTONE appears clutching a letter.

MRS JOHNSTONE *(singing):* We're startin' all over again.
DONNA MARIE *(speaking)* Is it a summons, Mother?
MRS JOHNSTONE *(singing):* Oh, bright new day,
 We're goin' away.
5 MICKEY *(calling):* Sammy!

MRS JOHNSTONE addresses various onlookers.

MRS JOHNSTONE *(singing):* Where nobody's heard our name.

SAMMY enters.

SAMMY *(speaking):* I never robbed nothin', honest, mam.
MRS JOHNSTONE *(singing):* Where we can begin again,
 Feel we can win and then
10 Live just like the livin' should be
 Got a new situation,
 A new destination,
 And no reputation following me.
 MICKEY *(speaking):* What is it, what is it?
15 MRS JOHNSTONE *(singing):* We're gettin' out,
 We're movin' house
 We're startin' all over again.
 We're leavin' this mess
 For our new address *(pointing it out)*
20 'Sixty five Skelmersdale Lane'.

MICKEY *(speaking; worried):* Where's that, mam?
SAMMY *(speaking):* Is that in the country?
DONNA MARIE *(speaking)* What's it like there?
MRS JOHNSTONE *(singing):* The air is so pure,
25   You get drunk just by breathing,
        And the washing stays clean on the line.
        Where there's space for the kids,
        'Cos the garden's so big,
        It could take you a week just to reach the far side.
30   *(Speaking):* Come on Sammy, Mickey, now you've all gorra help.
        (To the NEIGHBOURS in a 'posh' voice.) Erm would you excuse us,
        we've gorra pack. We're movin' away.

MRS JOHNSTONE and the children go in to pack.

NEIGHBOUR: What did she say?
MILKMAN: They're movin' away.
35 ALL: Praise the Lord, he has delivered us at last.
NEIGHBOUR: They're getting' out,
        They're movin' house,
        Life won't be the same as in the past.
POLICEMAN: I can safely predict
40   A sharp drop in the crime rate.
NEIGHBOUR: It'll be calm and peaceful round here.
MILKMAN: And now I might get even
        Get paid what is mine, mate.
NEIGHBOUR: An' you'll see, graffiti will soon disappear.

MRS JOHNSTONE marches out of the house carrying battered suitcases, followed by the children who are struggling to get out some of the items mentioned in the verse.

45 MRS JOHNSTONE: Just pack up the bags,
        We're leavin' the rags,
        The wobbly wardrobe, chest of drawers that never close.
        The two legged chair, the carpet so bare,
        You wouldn't see it if it wasn't for the holes.
50   Now that we're movin'
        Now that we're improvin'
        Let's just wash our hands of this lot.
        For it's no longer fitting for me to be sitting
        On a sofa, I know for a fact was knocked off.

The last line is delivered to Sammy who indicates the POLICEMAN, trying to get her to shut up.

55   We might get a car,
        Be all 'lardie dah'
        An' go drivin' out to the sands.
        At the weekend,
        A gentleman friend,
60   Might take me dancing
        To the local bands.
        We'll have a front room,

And then if it should happen,
That His Holiness flies in from Rome,
65   He can sit there with me, eating toast, drinking tea
In the sort of surroundings that remind him of home.
MICKEY *(speaking):* It's like the country, isn't it, mam?
MRS JOHNSTONE *(speaking):* Ey, we'll be all right out here son, away from all
     the muck an' the dirt an' the bloody trouble. Eh, I could dance. Come here.
70 MICKEY: Get off…

*MRS JOHNSTONE picks up a picture of the Pope which is lying next to one of the
     suitcases and begins to dance.*

MRS JOHNSTONE *(singing):* Oh, bright new day,
     We're movin' away
     We're startin' all over again.
     Oh bright new day,
75   We're goin' away,
     Where nobody's heard of our name.
     (Speaking): An' what are you laughin' at?
MICKEY: I'm not laughin', I'm smilin'. I haven't seen you happy like this for ages.
MRS JOHNSTONE: Well, I'm happy now. Eh, Jesus where's the others?
80 MICKEY: they went into that field, mam.
MRS JOHNSTONE: Sammy. SAMMY! Get off that bleedin' cow before I kill
     you. Oh Jesus, what's our Donna Marie stepped into. Sammy, that cow's a
     bull. Come here the pair of you.
     Now we can begin again,
85   Feel we can win an' then,
     Live just like the livin' should be.
     Got a new situation,
     A new destination
     An' no reputation following me.
90 ALL: We're getting' out. We're movin' house
     We're goin' away. Getting' out today.
     We're movin' movin' movin' house
MRS JOHNSTONE: We're goin' away,
     Oh, bright new day.

Kiki Dee as Mrs Johnstone,
Albery Theatre, London, 1988.

Share your thoughts with the rest of the class.

Moving On

Another feature of the play's structure is that it includes a narrator who talks directly to the audience. You are now going to consider the effect of using such a character. For most plays, the audience watches performances which are played out in front of them as if they were real-life incidents with real-life characters. With a narrator, the audience is reminded immediately that what they are watching is not real. What purposes, therefore does such a character serve?

A narrator is a useful device that a dramatist can use in several ways:

▶ to pass on information about plot, character or theme to the audience

▶ to act as a commentator for the writer in order to pass on his or her views, or to interpret what the audience is watching

▶ to inform the audience of the passage of time or a shift in the setting

▶ to challenge the audience to think about particular issues.

Look at the following lines spoken by the narrator and discuss the purpose of each speech.

One

NARRATOR *(speaking):* So did y' hear the story of the Johnstone twins?
  As like each other as two new pins,
  Of one womb born, on the self same day
  How one was kept and the other given away?
  And did you never hear how the Johnstones died,
  Never knowing that they shared one name,
  Till the day they died, when a mother cried
  My own dear sons lie slain.

Two

NARRATOR *(singing):* Did you really feel that you'd become secure,
  And that the past was safely locked away,
  Did you really feel that you would never be found?
  Did you forget you've got some debts to pay?
  Did you forget about the reckoning day?

  Yes the devil he's still got your number,
  He's moved in down the street from you,
  Someone said he wants to speak to you,
  Someone said they'd seen him leanin' on your door.

Three

There's a few bob in your pocket and you've got good friends,
And it seems that Summer's never coming to an end,
Young, free and innocent, you haven't got a care,
Apart from decidin' on the clothes you're gonna wear
The street's turned to Paradise, the radio's singing dreams
You're innocent, immortal, you're just fifteen.

The NARRATOR becomes the rifle range man at the fairground.

LINDA, MICKEY and EDWARD rush on.

*LINDA, MICKEY and EDWARD pool their money and hand it to the rifle range man.
He gives the gun to MICKEY, who smiles, shakes his head and points to LINDA. The man
offers the gun to EDWARD but LINDA takes it. The boys indicate to the rifle range man
that he has had it now LINDA has the gun. They eagerly watch the target but their smiles
fade as LINDA misses all three shots. MICKEY and EDWARD turn on LINDA in
mock anger. They are stopped by the rifle range man throwing them a coconut which is used for
a game of piggy-in-the-middle. When LINDA is caught in the middle the game freezes.*

And who'd dare tell the lambs in Spring,
What fate the lesser seasons bring?
Who'd tell the girl in the middle of the pair
The price she'll pay for just being there?

Share your responses with the rest of
the class.

Development

Using the notes you have made to help you,
write two paragraphs explaining:

▶ the **purpose** and **effect** of one of the songs
from the play

▶ how Willy Russell uses the narrator in one
of his speeches in the play.

Review

What have you learned about:

▶ the part that songs play in *Blood Brothers*?

▶ the role of the narrator?

Assignment Watch

An understanding of the structures and forms
used by the writer and how the action of the
play fits together will help you when you
come to assess the roles of the characters.

Step 5 – Staging a Key Scene

In this Step you are going to think about staging one of the scenes from the beginning of the play.

Mrs Johnstone has just learned that she is to have twins and is concerned that she will have difficulties in coping on the wages she earns. In this scene, Mrs Johnstone agrees to give one of her twins to Mrs Lyons, her employer, who is childless.

Starting Point

Read the scene and answer the questions on page 140.

MRS LYONS enters.

MRS LYONS: Hello, Mrs. J. How are you?

There is no reply.

(registering the silence) Mrs J? Anything wrong?
MRS JOHNSTONE: I had it all worked out.
MRS LYONS: What's the matter?
5   MRS JOHNSTONE: We were just getting straight.
MRS LYONS: Why don't you sit down
MRS JOHNSTONE: With one more baby we could have managed. But not with
      two. The Welfare have already been on to me. They say I'm incapable of
      controllin' the kids I've already got. They say I should put some of them
      into care. But I won't. I love the bones of everyone of them. I'll even love
10   these two when they come along. But like they say at the Welfare, kids
      can't live on love alone.
MRS LYONS: Twins? You're expecting twins?

The NARRATOR enters.

15 NARRATOR: How quickly an idea, planted, can
         Take root and grow into a plan.
         The thought conceived in this very room
         Grew as surely as a seed, in a mother's womb.

The Narrator exits.

MRS LYONS *(almost inaudibly)* Give one of them to me.
20 MRS JOHNSTONE: What?
MRS LYONS *(containing her excitement)*: Give one of them to me.
MRS JOHNSTONE: Give one to you?
MRS LYONS: Yes… yes.
MRS JOHNSTONE *(taking it almost as a joke)*: But y' can't just…
MRS LYONS: When are you due?
MRS JOHNSTONE: Erm, well about… Oh, but Mrs…
25 MRS LYONS: Quickly, quickly tell me… when are you due?
MRS JOHNSTONE: July he said, the beginning of…

MRS LYONS: July… and my husband doesn't get back until, the middle of July. He need never guess

30 MRS JOHNSTONE *(amused)* Oh, it's mad

MRS LYONS: I know it is. It's mad…but it's wonderful, it's perfect. Look, look, you're what, four months pregnant, but you're only just beginning to show… so, so I'm four months pregnant and I'm only just beginning to show. *(she grabs a cushion and arranges it beneath her dress.)* Look, look. I could

35 have got pregnant just before he went away. But I didn't tell him in case I miscarried, I didn't want to worry him whilst he was away. But when he arrives home I tell him we were wrong, the doctors were wrong. I have a baby, our baby. Mrs Johnstone, it will work, it will if only you'll…

MRS JOHNSTONE: Oh Mrs Lyons, you can't be serious.

40 MRS LYONS: You said yourself, you had too many children already.

MRS JOHNSTONE: Yeh, but I don't know if I wanna give one away.

MRS LYONS: Already you're being threatened by the Welfare people. Mrs Johnstone with two more children how can you possibly avoid some of them being put into care? Surely it's better to give one child to me. Look, at least if the child

45 was with me you'd be able to see him everyday, as you came to work.

MRS LYONS stares at MRS JOHNSTONE, willing her to agree.

Please Mrs Johnstone. Please.

MRS JOHNSTONE: Are y' … are y' that desperate to have a baby?

MRS LYONS *(singing):* Each day I look out from this window,
I see him with his friends, I hear him call,
50 I rush down but as I fold my arms around him,
He's gone, was he ever there at all?
I dreamed of all the places I would take him,
The games we'd play the stories I would tell,
The jokes we'd share, the clothing I would make him,
55 I reach out. But as I do. He fades away.

The melody shifts into that of MRS JOHNSTONE who is looking at MRS LYONS, feeling for her. MRS LYONS gives a half smile and a shrug, perhaps slightly embarrassed at what she has revealed. MRS JOHNSTONE turns and looks at the room she is in. Looking up in awe at the comparative opulence of and ease of the place. Tentatively and wondering she sings

MRS JOHNSTONE: If my child was raised
In a palace like this one,
(He) wouldn't have to worry where
His next meal was comin' from.
60 His clothing would be supplied by
George Henry Lee.

Mrs LYONS sees that MRS JOHNSTONE might be persuaded.

MRS LYONS *(singing)* He'd have all his own toys
And a garden to play in.

MRS JOHNSTONE: He could make too much noise
65 Without the neighbours complainin'.

MRS LYONS: Silver trays to take meals on

MRS JOHNSTONE: A bike with *both* wheels on?

MRS LYONS nods enthusiastically.

MRS LYONS: And he'd sleep every night
   In a bed of his own.

70 MRS JOHNSTONE: He wouldn't get into fights
   He'd leave matches alone.
   And you'd never find him
   Effin' and blindin'
   And when he grew up
75 He could never be told
   To stand and queue up
   For hours at the end of the dole
   He'd grow up to be
MRS LYONS/MRS JOHNSTONE: *(together)* A credit to me
80 MRS JOHNSTONE: To you.
MRS JOHNSTONE: I would still be able to see him every day, wouldn't I?
MRS LYONS: Of course.
MRS JOHNSTONE: An' …an' you would look after him, wouldn't y'?
MRS LYONS *(singing):* I'd keep him warm in the winter
85 And cool when it shines.
   I'd pull out his splinters
   Without making him cry.
   I'd always be there
   If his dream was a nightmare
90 My child.
   My child.

There is a pause before MRS JOHNSTONE nods. MRS LYONS goes across and kisses and hugs her. MRS JOHNSTONE is slightly embarrassed.

   Oh now you must help me. There's so much …. I'll have to … *(she takes out the cushion)* We'll do this properly so that it's thoroughly convincing, and I'll need to see you walk, and baby's clothes, I'll have to knit and buy bottles and suffer from piles.
95 MRS JOHNSTONE: what?
MRS LYONS: Doesn't one get piles when one's pregnant? And buy a cot and…Oh help me with this, Mrs J. Is it in the right place? *(She puts the cushion back again.)* I want it to look right before I go shopping.
100 MRS JOHNSTONE *(helping her with her false pregnancy):* What you goin' to the shops for? I do the shopping.
MRS LYONS: Oh no, from now on I do the shopping. I want everyone to know about my baby. *(She suddenly reaches for the Bible.)*

Music.

   Oh Mrs J … We must make this a, erm, a binding agreement.

Kiki Dee and Joanne Zorian as Mrs Johnstone and Mrs Lyons,
Albery Theatre, London, 1988.

1 How willing is Mrs Johnstone to give her child to Mrs Lyons?

2 What persuades Mrs Johnstone to agree? Think about: what Mrs Lyons says, what Mrs Johnstone says, and how Mrs Johnstone feels about Mrs Lyons.

3 Does Mrs Johnstone have any alternatives to giving up her child? Give reasons for your answer.

4 What do we learn about the social position of the two women from this scene?

Share your responses with the rest of the class.

Key Concept

The reasons why a character behaves in the way he or she does are what motivates him or her. In this scene you have been looking at Mrs Johnstone's and Mrs Lyon's **motivations**.

Moving On

Now you are going to think about the way that this scene could be staged. First, however, you need to consider what a director does in any production he or she is responsible for.

1 List the kinds of things that a director has to think about when he or she is preparing a drama text for production. For example, he or she will need to think about the characters' movements on stage, their gestures, make up and so on. What else needs to be considered? Try to come up with at least five points.

2 Share your thoughts with the rest of the class. Agree on a list of director's tasks.

Development

1 Now discuss how you will present the scene. Bearing in mind your responses to the questions you have just answered, you should:

  (i) consider how you will arrange the set for Mrs Lyons' home

 (ii) think about appearance of the characters. How will you show the difference in social class?

(iii) consider the role of the characters in the scene and how you would bring this out on stage

 (iv) identify any particularly important lines and decide how they should be spoken

  (v) interpret the stage directions given by the author and decide if or how you will follow them

 (vii) decide on the tone, type of voice, accent and gestures that the characters should use

(viii) determine any sound effects, special effects, extra props or music you would use – you must be able to explain why you have added these things (if you choose to do so) and how they add to your interpretation.

2 Summarise your thoughts for each of the above into a series of bullet points and be ready to report them to the class. Be sure that you can discuss the reasons for your staging decisions and interpretation of the characters.

Present your views to the rest of the class.

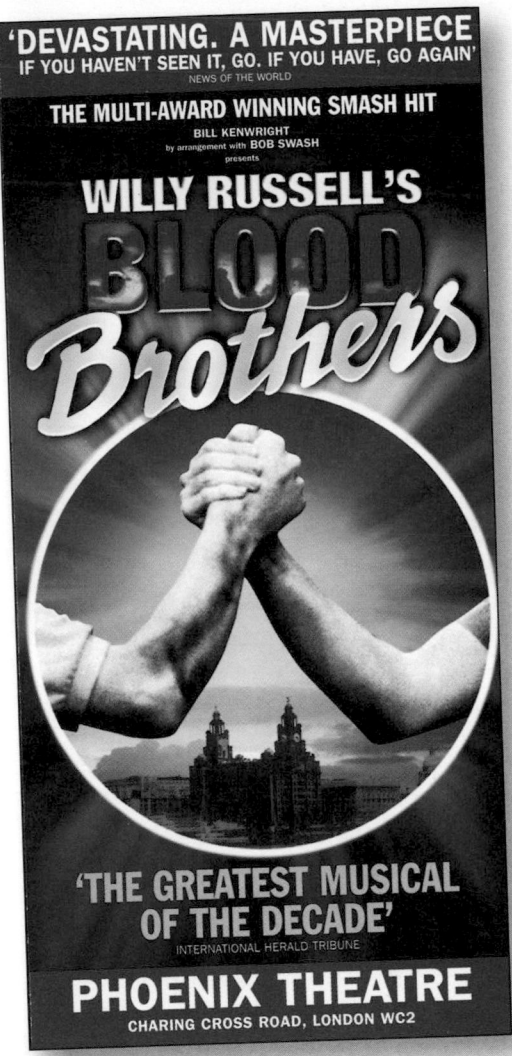

Review

What have you learned about the key issues a director must consider in staging a play?

Assignment Watch

The process of staging a play involves working on many issues. In this Step, you have learned about a director's role, the decisions s/he has to make and how they impact on the final performance.

Step 6 – Tackling the Assignment

It is now time to consider the GCSE Literature assignment; to choose a suitable task and to plan a response. This Step will help you with both of these activities.

Starting Point

Read the following questions.
Choose the assignment about which
you feel most confident.

Assignment 1

Write a letter from the director to the actor playing a character you have studied, in which you advise him or her about the role he or she will be playing and its importance to the play.

Assignment 2

Explain how a key scene from the play might be staged and explain the role of a chosen character in this part of the play.

Assignment 3

What is the role of your chosen character in the play?

Moving On

With other students working on the same assignment, discuss what you should include in your plan. Use the following grid to help you and make note of useful points.

Planning the assignment:		
Assignment	**Thinking:**	**Structure:**
1	This assignment requires you to focus on a character you have been studying and to give advice on how the character might be played by the actor. You must also look at the role of the character in the play. You should consider: the character's appearance, his or her personality, the impact of the social and historical setting in which the action takes place, the relationships with other characters, his or her movements and gestures and any important speeches and his or her role(s) in the play.	In your response, make sure that you: ▶ explain the aims and purpose of your writing ▶ describe the social and historical setting of the play and how this affects the character ▶ describe the appearance speech and motivation of the character and any changes they will undergo during the performance ▶ support your explanations with evidence from the play ▶ write in the appropriate form and register of a formal letter.

Planning the assignment:

Assignment	Thinking:	Structure:
2	This assignment asks you to look at a key scene you have studied. There are three important aspects to this task: A) you must cover carefully all of the staging issues that a director must consider in preparing a production of your key scene. B) you should consider the role of your chosen character in this scene. C) you should describe how you would represent social and historical issues in this scene. You should think about: the stage set; the appearance of the characters; the role of the character that you have been studying; the important lines and how they should be spoken; any stage directions in the text and how you would interpret them; the tone, register and gestures that the characters should use; any sound effects, special effects, props or music you would use.	In your response, make sure that you: ▶ explain the aims and purpose of your writing ▶ analyse the impact of the social and historical issues on the play as a whole and on this scene in particular ▶ cover all the aspects of staging systematically ▶ discuss the role of your chosen character in the scene ▶ support your ideas by referring closely to the text.

Planning the assignment:

Assignment	Thinking:	Structure:
3	This assignment requires you to consider the role of your chosen character in the whole of the play. You will need to focus on: ▶ his or her personality and character ▶ the way the author uses the character to convey his or her thoughts ▶ the way the character is used to explore and/or represent the social and historical issues of the time.	Use any notes you have made, and in your response, make sure that you: ▶ explain the aims and purpose of your writing; ▶ write in detail about the kind of character the author has created, covering his or her personality, background, environment and relationships ▶ write about the role(s) he or she fulfils in the play ▶ make sure that you demonstrate clear understanding of issues raised by the social and historical context of the play and the author's viewpoint of them ▶ refer closely to the text to support your claims.

❨Development❩

Complete your plan.

❨Review❩

What have you learned about:

▶ the requirements of these assignments?

▶ planning a Literature response?

Boost Your Grade

Starting Point

Look at the grade criteria that the examiner will use to assess your work. Make a note of anything that you do not understand.

English Criteria Checklist		
Grade E	**Grade C**	**Grade A**
A Familiarity when describing: ▶ what we learn about a character from dialogue, action and the kind of language he or she uses ▶ the dramatic devices and the impact they are intended to have on an audience ▶ the text's social and historical setting.	Show insight when discussing: ▶ what we learn about a character from dialogue, action and the kind of language he or she uses ▶ the dramatic devices and the impact they are intended to have on an audience ▶ ideas and themes ▶ the text's social and historical context and the literary tradition on which it draws. ▶ how different meanings are conveyed through structure and form	Show analytical and interpretative skills when evaluating: ▶ the intended effects of character and action ▶ the layers of meaning in language, ideas and themes ▶ the impact of the social and historical setting on the text ▶ the effects of dramatic devices or structures ▶ alternative approaches and interpretations.

Discuss any concerns you may have about the criteria with your teacher.

Moving On

1 Read the following extracts by two students writing about the plays they have studied, and the assessor's comments that follow:

2 Find evidence from each excerpt to support the assessor's comments.

Excerpt 1

In this extract, the writer is responding to the first assignment on Blood Brothers.
This is part of the letter that he or she writes to the actor playing the part of Mrs Johnstone. In it, the writer is dealing with the character's background and appearance.

> The play begins with a song, 'Marilyn Monroe'. Willy Russell introduces Mrs Johnstone to the audience and it is obvious that she is a working-class mother. She has been left by her husband to struggle with a large family. Her looks are already beginning to fade. The words tell us that:
>
> By the time that I was 25, I looked like 42.
>
> Her lifestyle and lack of money have had an effect on her looks. She had been a stunning blonde and soon met and married her husband when she became pregnant. Now, several years later, she is wrinkled and tired. Her figure is now poorly dressed and 'twice the size of Marilyn Monroe', and she is heavily pregnant. (The moment she speaks it is obvious she is from Liverpool because of her strong accent.) We get the impression that she has been an easy-going girl with a poor education who has been used and who has now been rejected so that her hopes and dreams have been broken. She lives with the memories of 'dancing' as a girl and with little chance of things getting better. All of this is clear from her appearance and the very first song of the play, encouraging the audience to feel sympathetic towards her.

Assessor's Comment

This extract shows the student **discussing the character's role**. He or she understands that Mrs Johnstone is the product of the lifestyle she has been forced to lead. There is some evidence that **he or she empathises with** the character's situation. Whilst there is some reference to text in support of the student's comments and an **understanding of the impact Russell wants the character to have on the audience**, there is only **limited reference** to the text's social and historical context. This student meets the majority of the criteria for a Grade C for Literature.

This extract is from a response to assignment 3 for
An Inspector Calls. At this point, the student is writing
about the role of Arthur Birling as a capitalist.

All of Priestley's reservations about capitalism are reflected in Birling's character. He is portrayed as a hard, inflexible and uncaring employer, who is motivated by profit and expanding his business empire. His drive for 'lower costs and higher prices' confirms how little he considers the social impact of his decisions on his workforce. The fact that he views his daughter's marriage to Gerald Croft as an opportunity for a business merger is not only unfeeling but a clear insight to the way he thinks. Given the reason for the celebratory dinner that evening, his daughter Sheila's engagement, the audience is struck by the inappropriateness of Birling's main concern that 'we may look forward to the time when Crofts and Birlings are no longer competing but are working together'. These characteristics, combined with Birling's pompous and overbearing nature, are clear indications of Priestley's contempt for capitalism. The timing of the Inspector's arrival is deliberate and designed to cut Birling short and allow the opportunity to expose his opinions to close 'inspection'.

Assessor's Comment

This is clearly a very able candidate who is able to **analyse, interpret and evaluate** the way in which the playwright is **using the character's role to voice his own political viewpoint** by exposing Birling's to critical scrutiny. He or she is able to support his or her comments with **selective and appropriate references to the text**. In this part of the response, the student **touches on the social and historical setting of the text** in that he or she understands how Birling's attitude might impact on working class people. This candidate is working at Grade A/A* for Literature.

Share your responses with the rest of
the class.

Development

Below are two extracts of students' writing about the drama text they have studied. One was awarded a Grade A, the other a grade E.

Read the extracts and use the prompts that follow to write a commentary on each piece.

Excerpt 3

This is a short excerpt taken from a response to the third assignment on Blood Brothers, *concerning the character's role in the play. In it, the student is writing about what he or she sees as the author's wish to explain and not criticise the struggle that some single mothers have to bring up their children.*

Willy Russell uses Mrs Johnstone to make several of the points about life that he wishes to make clear in his musical Blood Brothers. First, as a single mother, Mrs Johnstone represents all those women who have been left with all the responsibility of raising a family and who are often criticised by society. There is undoubtedly a feeling that children from single-parent homes are harmed by the lack of control of the mother. The narrator describes Mrs Johnstone as having 'a stone' in the place of her heart. He is suggesting that she is hard and cold and lets her family down. Willy Russell, however, allows us to see the real struggle of such a woman. She has no money, no time and no support, but she does the best she can. We learn that she 'loves the bones' of every one of her children but that she is also the victim of an irresponsible husband who left her, and a society that fails to support her financially. She is forced to live on hire purchase from catalogues, or the 'never, never' as she calls it, and to do the best she can.

Excerpt 4

In this extract, the writer is responding to the second assignment on
An Inspector Calls. *In it, the student is writing about the staging of a key
scene and the role of Arthur Birling. At this point he or she is writing about
the way that the set should reflect the social context of the early 1900s.*

I would want the stage to look like a dining room owned by rich people. The Birling family have lots of money and the room should show this. It should have a big, carved table with candles and expensive knives and forks. The walls of the room would be covered in expensive-looking paper and there would be a big glass chandelier hanging over the table. There would also be lots of pictures of important-looking people and a big sideboard. The furniture would probably be dark and heavy. All of these things are important because I want to get across the fact that the Birlings have plenty of money and think that they are better than other people. The house is not a place where you would feel very relaxed.

1 Use these prompts to help you to write a commentary on each extract:

(i) Identify the point(s) each of the writers makes. Is each point clear and carefully explained?

(ii) Are the points supported by evidence from the text? Is there sufficient evidence?

(iii) Do the students develop each point sufficiently to make their meaning clear?

(iv) Do they use the appropriate formal register and tone for a literature assignment?

(v) Which set of grade criteria best fits each student's work?

2 Write a commentary on each extract using the following headings:

▶ strengths;

▶ use of evidence

▶ register and tone

▶ areas for improvement.

Original Writing

Objectives

In successfully completing this unit, you will:

▶ read two types of original writing: personal writing and narrative

▶ identify the key features of these types of writing

▶ prepare a plan for a piece of original writing

▶ draft, revise and proofread your writing

▶ present your final piece of work for GCSE assessment.

GCSE

You will:

▶ complete a GCSE Speaking and Listening component – giving an individual talk

▶ complete a GCSE Writing assignment

▶ develop the skills you need for the GCSE examination.

Coursework and Examination Skills

▶ *Reading* – analytical reading of fiction

▶ *Writing* – writing to explore, imagine or entertain

▶ *Speaking and Listening* – working co-operatively with others in a group discussion.

Step 1 – Personal Writing: Clare's Painful Experience

Starting Point

The successful completion of any assignment depends upon a clear understanding of what it involves. You are, therefore, going to begin this unit by:

a) defining the word 'original' in 'original writing'

b) agreeing on the features that make a 'good' piece of original writing.

Working with a partner, agree a one-sentence definition of the word 'original', which you are prepared to share with the class.

Discuss some of the definitions your classmates have given and agree on a 'working' definition that is clear and that outlines the meaning of 'original' in simple terms.

Use the agreed definition to create a spidergram of different types of original writing. Here are a couple of ideas to help you:

1 As a class, compare your conclusions and create a joint spidergram of all the types of original writing.

2 Think about what makes a piece of original writing engaging or entertaining. List five features of 'good' original writing. For example, an interesting opening or a good description.

3 Decide which of these features are common to all types of original writing, and which are specific to particular types.

Moving On

The two most common forms of original writing are personal (often autobiographical) and narrative (fictional story writing). Now that you have considered what in general makes writing successful and powerful, you are going to examine personal writing more closely.

Clare is a Year 11 student whose class has been looking at a number of readings under the heading 'Good Times, Bad Times'. When Clare was asked to write about an incident from her childhood, she chose to write a vivid description of the day she broke her arm.

As you read this story, bear in mind the features of successful writing you have already discussed. How many of them can you identify?

A Painful Experience

If I had not been worried about being late, if I had taken the time to tie my shoelace, if I had walked instead of running, it would never have happened. Looking back now, it is easy to see how it could have been avoided. But, typically, I did worry, I did run and I did not see the boy in front of me until it was too late. There was impact, a minor collision really, but enough to send me crashing to the floor and enough to shatter my left arm.

It was five past one, the bell had rung at one o'clock for the end of lunch. I had been busy, rehearsing the school play when it sounded. With the benefit of hindsight, I am sure that my teacher would have understood if I had been a few minutes late for registration, but, when you are ten years old, your confidence in the kindness of teachers is less secure. I decided to hurry; a poor decision.

I was running behind everyone else and my shoelace was flapping against my leg. I called to Anne and Catherine to ask them to wait as I was concerned that I might lose my shoe. But they ignored me and I was forced to carry on to catch them. I was totally oblivious of the people in front of me as I hurtled on. Then, in mid stride, my shoelace snagged under the heel of a boy I was overtaking and I stopped suddenly, overbalanced and fell awkwardly with only enough time to put my arm out to break my fall.

For a moment I was in a daze. I could not see or hear a thing. Like a cartoon character, with birds twittering around my head, I felt nothing. I was stunned. Then the pain flared; a kind of searing knife wound, a burning, throbbing agony that obliterated any other feeling I had. My left arm was twisted, misshapen and mangled. I could not think clearly. I felt cold and yet the sweat was already pouring from me. Finally my brain engaged once more and I let out a blood-curdling scream.

I cried and cried and cried. My friend, Anne, helped me to the washroom to clean up my cuts. Little did she know that it was not my grazed knee that was the problem. I tried to tell her but my sobs made my speech garbled. Then the headteacher arrived to see what all the fuss was about. A close examination resulted in more pain, but the support of a sling did help a little. His face told me all I needed to know about his diagnosis. He suspected that I had fractured my arm. I hoped that he was wrong but feared that he was right.

Luckily my mother is a teacher at the school and she was able to rush me to the Casualty Department at the nearby hospital for an x-ray. By the time I arrived at the hospital I was in a terrible state.

40 Every bump in the road sent the pain shuddering from my wrist to my elbow. I could taste the salt tears on my lips. Once inside the hospital corridor, the stench of disinfectant made me retch. I was exhausted and longed for my bed.

45 We filled in forms and waited in featureless rooms. I was in so much pain that I tried to read the posters on the walls to take my mind off my problem. Anything was better than thinking of six centimetres of bone that ached even if I stayed perfectly still. Four centuries later, I was ushered into the doctor's room. He needed all of two seconds to confirm my worst fears and I was rushed to x-ray in 50 a wheelchair. In all, I had five x-rays, each from a different and more excruciating angle. From there, I was taken to the children's ward to await the operation I needed to correct my fracture.

Twenty minutes after I had my first painkilling injection, my father arrived. It had worked very well and I greeted my dad like a distant 55 cousin arriving for a birthday tea.

"Hi, Dad, I'm glad you could make it."

He smiled, slightly relieved. He was worried, but the nonchalance of my greeting amused him.

Then my mind turned once more to what lay ahead. I was very 60 worried before I went for my operation. I was collected by a porter and wheeled out of the ward, flanked by my mum and dad. My mum looked anxious and my dad made bad jokes to try to lighten the mood. I left them standing together as I was wheeled into the theatre. As soon as I had been given the anaesthetic, I tried to count: ten, nine, 65 eight oblivion! An hour later, it was over and my arm was encased in plaster. It ached relentlessly and it felt heavy and yet fragile, but I did feel a little better and I slipped into a deep sleep until morning.

Luckily things got better day by day as the healing process took over. However, even now, when I think of that day in November, I experience 70 a certain clamminess and an empty feeling in the pit of my stomach. I remember the sickening crack, the searing pain and the coarse salty taste of my tears. I shiver and turn my thoughts to other, more pleasant memories, and I try to forget the day that I first felt real pain!

Now, you are going to examine the features in more detail through closer reading of Clare's text.

1 Look at the first paragraph. How does Clare gain the interest of the reader? Think about:

◗ how and when she reveals what happened to her

◗ her sentence openings

◗ her use of punctuation.

2 Look at the remaining paragraphs. How does Clare develop her story line?

Think about:

▶ the sequence of events (making a brief note of the event(s) each paragraph covers will help you)

▶ the things she leaves out as well as what she tells us

▶ how the writing style enables the reader to share Clare's experiences

▶ how she suggests the passing of time.

3 Look at the final paragraph. How does the story end? Is it effective? Think about when the incident actually happened and how the experience has affected Clare.

Share your conclusions with the rest of the class.

Development

You are now going to be working with words and sentences. Here is part of the commentary written by the teacher who assessed Clare's work.

1 Read what it says.

"This writing contains several features which make it effective and engaging. In particular, the student's choice of imaginative verbs and adjectives, similes and repetition deepen the reader's understanding of events and the writer's thoughts and feelings. The occasional use of short sentences adds impact to the writing."

2 Find some evidence that supports the teacher's comments. Make lists of examples of verbs, adjectives, similes, repetition and short sentences. If you are working with a photocopy of Clare's writing, you could use colour to highlight the examples that you find.

Share your findings with the rest of the class.

Next, you are going to apply some of what you have learned to your own writing. First turn to page 163 and choose one of the options for personal writing listed under section 1a) to g). Draft the first 100 words of the assignment (which is equivalent to the first three paragraphs of Clare's piece). This work will save you time when you come to write your final assignment and may also be used as the basis for a GCSE speaking and listening assessment.

Review

List at least five of the skills that Clare has used to create a powerful account of an apparently minor event.

1 Discuss a definition of 'original writing'.

2 Talk about the features of original writing.

3 How successful is the given example in meeting the criteria for successful writing you drew up earlier in the lesson?

Assignment Watch

In this Step you have considered the elements of original writing that may make it effective and powerful. You have concentrated on personal writing and how the use of certain devices helps to make it vivid and entertaining. These devices include adjectives, similes, repetition, short sentences and an attention-grabbing opening.

Starting Point

In the first part of this unit you studied a piece of personal writing. You are now going to look at another form of original writing, narrative.

What follows is a story about Jack, who takes a break from some of the stresses in his personal and professional life by escaping into the Cornish countryside for a few days. However, what was meant to be a relaxing time, did not quite go according to plan…

1 Before reading all of the short story 'Dinner at Eight' printed below, look quickly at the first paragraph. What narrative voice is being used? Compare this with the voice used in Clare's story.

2 What do you think the effect will be of using the chosen voice in 'Dinner at Eight'?

3 Now read the rest of 'Dinner at Eight'.

Dinner at Eight

"At last!"

Jack was a little surprised at the sound of his own voice. The relief at finding the guesthouse came through very clearly. He had forgotten how clogged the country lanes of Cornwall became once you had left the A-roads.

5   The drive had taken a lot longer than he had planned. The directions he had been given were not too good – twice he had taken wrong turns – but, finally, Tor View appeared in the headlights of the car. He had hoped to arrive early enough to take a brief walk onto the moors before his evening meal. As it was, he would just about have enough time to take his bag to his room, wash and get down to the dining

10 room. Mrs Lumsden had sounded very nice on the telephone, but she had insisted that dinner would be served at eight o'clock sharp. There had been something in the way she had said 'sharp' that suggested she didn't expect him to be late, and Jack was there to relax, not annoy the landlady.

    The last six months had been really hard going at the office. All he wanted now

15 was to get away from it all for a few days and wind down. No work, mobile switched off, some easy reading – four days with nothing to do but rest and breathe fresh air.

    He parked in one of the spaces at the side of the house, grabbed his bag from the boot and rang the doorbell. When she answered, Mrs Lumsden wasn't exactly the way he had pictured her – a little taller and not quite so plump, but definitely with the open,

20 friendly face. She could have been anywhere between 60 and 75, Jack was not good at fixing people's ages. The formalities were quickly dealt with. It didn't surprise him that he was the only guest at this time of year, but that was okay with him.

    He hadn't realised how hungry he was. The meal was simple but good home cooking, and a lot better than the fast food he had resorted to recently. Mrs

25 Lumsden, her name was Eunice but Mrs Lumsden seemed more appropriate, joined him at the table and they chatted easily. He worked in an advertising agency…well paid…lots of pressure…lived alone…most recent failed relationship with Kirsten. He didn't go into too much detail, just enough to keep things moving. She had kept the

guesthouse on after her husband died five years ago – mainly for something to do as she didn't need the money now – and she met some very nice people, you know!

"Do you have anything particular you want to do while you're here, Mr Murray?"

"Not really. I just need a break. You know, recharge the batteries. Eat some of your good food. Do some reading. Lots of sleep. Who knows? Maybe a casual walk before dinner."

"There are some lovely walks around here. But be careful where you go. The moors are riddled with old tin-mine shafts. Very dangerous if you don't have your wits about you."

"Don't worry. I don't intend going too far. I'm a stroller, not a hiker."

"Well, just be careful, my dear."

The next three days slipped into an easy pattern. Up ready for breakfast at 9am, then into the garden to make the best of the late autumn sun – not hot but pleasantly warm – and lose himself in a book. For lunch (his arrangement with Mrs Lumsden was bed, breakfast and evening meal), he drove the three miles into Bilston to take a bar snack in The Blacksmith's Arms. Afterwards, he wandered around the town, calling in on the book, craft and antique shops that bustled during the summer but were much quieter at the end of October. Returning to Tor View at around three, he went to his room to read and catnap until around 5.30pm, at which time he showered and dressed for his pre-dinner walk. Just the thing to sharpen his appetite. The only slight variation was that each evening he wandered a little further into the moor before turning back. However, he was always mindful of the mineshafts and he was always back by eight o'clock. After dinner, he turned in at ten and slept long and deep. Just what he needed.

The fourth day was no different – until he was out on the moor. As it was his last night, his mind was drawn towards what would be awaiting him. The Bradburn chocolate campaign needed some finishing touches before presenting it to the clients the week after next; the new Webster account was likely to come his way – very big, very demanding; catch up on mail (both kinds); check his messages (he was pleased he had kept his promise not to 'touch base' – his mobile was in his bag back at Tor View, where it had been since he arrived). Then there was Kirsten. Was it possible to put things back together with her? Was there any point in trying?

It was the pain of that thought that brought his attention back to the present and he realised that he had wandered a lot further than intended. He would have to hurry to get back in time for dinner. He took a moment to collect his thoughts and tried to picture the most direct route to Tor View. He set off a brisk pace in anticipation of his last meal with Mrs Lumsden.

Perhaps it was his haste. Perhaps his thoughts were elsewhere. Whatever the cause, he was suddenly aware of the ground giving way beneath his feet. As he began to slide, Mrs Lumsden's first night warning flashed into his mind. Frantically, he dug his heels into the side wall and grabbed at anything that might hold his weight. Twice he thought he had managed to stop himself but each time the tufts of scrubby grass gave way and he slid over the edge. With increasing urgency, he thrashed about wildly to find anything that would save him from tumbling who knew how far to what must be certain death.

It was his right hand that found the root of some surface bush and he thankfully clutched at it. It held his weight and, as he dangled, he tried to gather his wits.

When he looked up, he could see the rim of the hole some two or three metres above him. Looking down, there was nothing but blackness. Very slowly, he shifted his body position to find a toehold to take some of the strain from his arms, but as he did so he felt the root begin to loosen just a little. He couldn't risk trying to pull himself up in case it gave way altogether. All he could think to do was keep as still as possible and shout for help, though he wasn't hopeful as he hadn't met anyone on any of his previous walks. Though the night air was cold, sweat ran down his back. Every time he called out, he listened for a response. None came.

Thoughts churned through his head. This was definitely not the way he had ever seen himself dying. Who would miss him? Parents? Yes. Brother? Yes, though they weren't close. Graham and Mike? Yes – they were good friends. Tony, Al, Pam at the agency? Probably – for a while at least. Kirsten? He'd like to think so – but? If ever he got out of this mess, he would do something about Kirsten.

Time and again, he called out. Time and again, nothing but silence. Holding his body still was uncomfortable and the strain was tiring. He began to think this really might be the end. Once more, he raised his voice and listened. At first came the expected silence, but then he thought he heard a voice. He strained to listen. The numbness of his body was spreading to his mind. Was it playing tricks on him? No! There it was again. Definitely a voice. A man's voice. And, as he looked up, he could see the beam of a torch cutting through the darkness.

He allowed himself to hope and the hope gave strength to his voice.

"Here! Help! Over here!"

Moments later he was closing his eyes against the brightness of torch light. But the discomfort of that was nothing to the relief he felt as he heard, "I'll have you out of there in a jiffy" drift down to him. The light moved to the side and a rope was lowered to him. At first, he hesitated, unsure of letting go of the root that had saved him. Then he roused himself, took a firm grip and allowed himself to be hauled to the surface. Two large, strong hands lifted him clear and laid him on solid ground. While he tried to massage some feeling back into his limbs and sip the hot, sweet tea he had been handed, he heard his rescuer talking on a mobile.

"I've got him Mrs Lumsden. Yes, he'll be fine. Over by Lesser Ghyll. Very lucky I'd say. Will you let the others know? About 30 to 40 minutes I should think. Right, see you then."

He turned his attention back to Jack.

"Now, Mr Murray, are you ready?"

"When you are, Mr…?"

"Garvey. Bob Garvey. Call me Bob."

"Ready when you are, Bob. And thanks for finding me."

"It's like this, Mr Murray, when Mrs Lumsden says, 'Come quick', that's what we do."

"What made her call you?"

"You were late for dinner!"

As cold and tired as he was, Jack had to smile at that.

"Before we go Bob, may I borrow your torch?"

"Why?"

"I have to see into that hole."

"If you want. But there's not much to see."

"I just have to see the danger I was in."

Jack wasn't certain, but he thought he saw a little smile on Bob's face as he took the torch from his hand. He stepped to the rim, prepared himself and looked over.
125 He wasn't sure what to expect, but what he saw shocked him. The hole was, maybe, three metres across; the walls almost vertical. He could make out the root that had saved him and, from what he could see, it was the only thing that might have broken his fall. To that extent, he had been very lucky. What really surprised him was the realisation that the bottom was only about one or two metres below where he had
130 been hanging from the root. He turned to Bob, who stood watching him.

"I feel such an idiot, dragging you out to rescue me from that."

"Even if you'd known, you couldn't have got out on your own. Anyway, that isn't the real problem. Let's go."

Feeling a little foolish, Jack fell into step with Bob.
135 They had only gone about twenty paces when Bob suddenly yelled, "Stop!" and grabbed Jack's arm.

"Look!"

Jack followed the line of the torch. He was looking at a hole much like the other but here, the torch could not pick out the bottom.
140 "Lesser Ghyll. Over 25 metres straight down. This is where you were heading. No one comes up from here in one piece."

Jack peered onto the blackness.

"May I borrow your phone, Bob? There is someone I have to call. Right now!"

Moving On

Unlike Clare's story, 'Dinner at Eight' is entirely fictitious. Writing of this kind involves the author in a great deal of thought even before the first draft is written.

The following tasks should enable you to identify what the writer set out to convey to his audience.

Spend about ten minutes discussing one of the following. (If you are working with a photocopy of the story, you could use colour to highlight what you find.)

❰Setting❱

1 Make a list of words or phrases used to describe the place where the story happens.

2 Identify which part of speech (nouns, verbs, adjectives, adverbs) each word is.

3 How has the writer managed to create such a clear impression of the setting using so few adverbs and adjectives?

❰Character❱

4 Make a list of words or phrases that tell us anything about Jack or Mrs Lumsden. Think about their personalities and interests.

5 What makes each of them behave the way he or she does?

6 Use the information you have noted to create a pen picture or brief character study that you can share with the class.

❰Plot❱

You will notice that the story is written in the order in which it happens, with events spread over several days. This presents the writer with the challenge of showing the passage of time.

7 List or highlight all the words and phrases which show that time has passed.

8 From your list, choose three or four examples and discuss alternatives that could have been used.

9 If the writer had chosen to tell this story out of sequence, how might it have been done? Would it have been better? Give reasons for your answer.

(Structure)

You might have observed that information about the plot, setting and characters is not presented through long descriptions. For example, there are no passages about the Cornish countryside or about the characters. Instead, the writer chooses to spread details throughout the story. For example in the second paragraph the writer tells us something about the journey, the landscape and Mrs Lumsden's personality. By re-reading the first page of the story, you will see how this works.

10 What are the advantages and drawbacks of writing in this way?

Feed back your group's finding to the rest of the class.

(Development)

Look at lines 84 to 88 and 93 to 94. Here the writer is concentrating on Jack's thoughts as he faces possible death. At this point, he is reflecting both on his past and on his present situation. The writer uses a number of stylistic devices to help the reader to understand what Jack is going through. You are now going to work out what these are.

1 How does the writer use punctuation to emphasise Jack's thoughts?

2 The writer deliberately breaks the rules governing sentences. How many non-sentences can you find? Why does he do this?

3 There are many short sentences in the story. What effect does using so many short sentences have on the reader?

4 Talk about what you find with the rest of the class.

5 Now you are going to apply some of what you have learned to your own writing. Look at the two options 2a) and b) for narrative writing given on pages 163–164. Draft the next 200 words of one of the short stories, making sure that you:

▶ introduce the characters

▶ set them in their context

▶ work up to the turning point of the story.

This work will save you time when you come to write your final assignment.

(Review)

What have you learned about narrative writing? Think about:

▶ planning

▶ structure

▶ stylistic devices.

(Assignment Watch)

In this Step you have considered the elements of narrative that may make it effective and powerful. In particular you have looked at voice, setting, character, plot, structure and length.

Starting Point

In this unit you have now examined a piece of personal writing and a piece of narrative. Both examples use language to convey vivid physical description at important points in the writing. Look back at lines 22 to 28 in 'A Painful Experience' and lines 74 to 83 in 'Dinner at Eight'.

1 How do the writers make their characters' experiences seem more real?

2 Think about how they refer to the five senses. Support your answers with examples from the text.

Share your findings with the rest of the class.

Moving On

You will now read an extract from the novel *A Kestrel for a Knave* by Barry Hines. Although the whole novel is an example of fictional writing, the extract tells a 'story within a story'. In it you will find many of the devices that you have explored through the previous two pieces in this unit. The extract is set in an English lesson in a secondary school. One of the boys, Anderson, tells the class about something that happened when he was younger.

As you read the extract, think about how the five senses are used to make the story vivid.

A Kestrel for a Knave

He swung one arm and indicated the board behind him. On it was printed:
FACT AND FICTION

"What did we say fact was, Armitage?"

"Something that's happened, Sir."

5   "Right. Something that has happened. Something that we know is real. The things that we read about in the newspapers, or hear on the news. Events, accidents, meetings; the things that we see with our own eyes, the things all about us; all these are facts. Have you got that? Is that clear?"

Chorus: "Yes, Sir."

10   "Right then. Now if I asked Anderson for some facts about himself, what could he tell us?"

"Sir! Sir!"

"All right! All right! Just put your hands up. There's no need to jump down my throat. Jordan?"

15   "He's wearing jeans."

"Good Mitchell?"

"He's got black hair."

"Yes. Fisher?"

"He lives down Shallowbank Crescent."

20   "Do you, Anderson?"

"Yes, Sir."

"Right then. Now all these are facts about Anderson, but they're not particularly interesting facts. Perhaps Anderson can tell us something about himself that is interesting. A really interesting fact."

25   There was a massive "Woooo!" from the rest of the class. Mr Farthing grinned and rode it; then he raised his hands to control it.

"Quietly now. Quietly."

The class quietened, still grinning. Anderson stared at his desk, blushing.

"I don't know owt, Sir."

30   "Anything at all Anderson, anything that's happened to you, or that you've seen which sticks in your mind."

"I can't think of owt, Sir."

"What about when you were little? Everybody remembers something about when they were little. It doesn't have to be fantastic, just something that you've

35 remembered."

Anderson began to smile and looked up.

"There's summat. It's nowt though."

"It must be if you remember it."

"It's daft really."

40   "Well tell us then, and let's all have a laugh."

"Well it was once when I was a kid. I was at Junior school, I think, or somewhere like that, and went down to Fowlers Pond, me and this other kid. Reggie Clay they called him, he didn't come to this school; he flitted and went away somewhere. Anyway it was spring, tadpole time, and it's swarming with

45   tadpoles down there in spring. Edges of t'pond are all black with 'em, and me and this other kid started to catch 'em. It was easy, all you did, you just put your hands together and scooped a handful of tadpoles. Anyway we were mucking about with 'em, picking 'em up and chucking 'em back and things, and we were on about taking some home, but we'd no jam jars. So this kid,

50   Reggie, says, 'Take thi' wellingtons off and put some in there, they'll be all right 'til tha gets home.' So I took 'em off and we put some water in 'em and then we started to put taddies in 'em. We kept ladling 'em in and I says to this kid, 'Let's have a competition, thee have one welli' and I'll have t'other, and we'll see who can get most in!' So he started to fill one welli' and I started to

55   fill t'other. We must have been at it hours, and they got thicker and thicker, until at t'end there was no water left in 'em, they were just jam packed wi'taddies.

"You ought to have seen 'em, all black and shiny, right up to t'top. When we'd finished we kept dipping us fingers into 'em and whipping 'em up at each

60   other, all shouting and excited like. Then this kid says to me, 'I bet tha daren't put one on.' And I says, 'I bet tha daren't.' So we said we'd put one on each. We wouldn't though, we kept reckoning to, then running away, so we tossed up and him who lost had to do it first. And I lost, oh, and you'd to take your socks off an' all. So I took my socks off, and kept looking at this welli' full of

65   taddies, and this kid kept saying, 'Go on then, tha frightened, tha frightened.' I was an' all. Anyway I shut my eyes and started to put my foot in. Oooo. It was just like putting your feet into live jelly. They were frozen. And when my foot went down, they all came over t'top of my wellington, and when I got my foot to t'bottom, I could feel 'em all squashing about between my toes.

70   "Anyway, I'd done it, and I says to this kid, "Thee put thine on now.' But he wouldn't, he was dead scared, so I put it on instead. I'd got used to it then, it was all right after a bit; it sent your legs all excited and tingling like. When I'd got 'em both on I started to walk up to this kid, waving my arms and making spook noises; and as I walked they all came squelching over t'tops again and

75   ran down t'sides. This kid looked frightened to death, he kept looking at my wellies so I tried to run at him and they all spurted up my legs. You ought to have seen him. He just screamed out and ran home roaring.

"It was a funny feeling though when he'd gone; all quiet, with nobody there, and up to t'knees in tadpoles."

80   Silence. The class up to their knees in tadpoles.

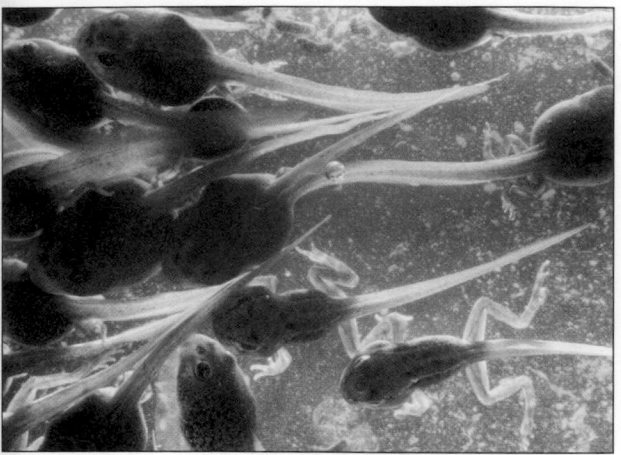

2 What effect does the use of local dialect give to the story? Give reasons for your answer.

3 Anderson alternates between quoted dialogue, or direct speech (e.g. 'I bet tha daren't' in line 61) and reported speech (e.g. 'So we said we'd put one on each' in line 61). Find another example of each.

4 What effect do such choices have on the storytelling? Think about:

▶ the character who is speaking

▶ other characters who are being discussed

▶ how the writer provides information that helps the story develop.

◀ **Using the Five Senses** ▶

1 What does the writer mean when he says the class were 'up to their knees in tadpoles' in the last line?

2 How has this been achieved by Anderson?

◀ **Using Detail** ▶

Mr Farthing first says that the facts that others give about Anderson are 'not particularly interesting'. Within Anderson's story, however, he uses many apparently minor details. For example of where Reggie Clay went to school.

1 Find five more details that he includes.

2 What effect does this detail have on his personal account?

◀ **Development** ▶

A *Kestrel for a Knave* is set in Barnsley, and the characters often speak in the local dialect rather than Standard English

1 Make a list of local words used in the extract and give the Standard English equivalent. For example, 'owt' is local dialect. If you were using Standard English, you would use 'anything' instead.

◀ **Review** ▶

Look back at the written work you have drafted in Steps 1 and 2 in response to some of the coursework assignment options at the end of the unit. Incorporate what you have learned in this Step about describing the senses and/or using speech.

What are the main effects of:

▶ using reference to the five senses in descriptive language?

▶ using dialect/non-Standard English?

▶ using dialogue?

◀ **Assignment Watch** ▶

In this Step you have looked at some further stylistic devices which are often used both in narrative and personal writing. In particular, you have examined the use of language to evoke the five senses, and the language spoken by characters.

Step 4 – Tackling the Assignment

Starting Point

In this Step, you are going to select a writing task and start the planning phase.

Before looking at the assignments, briefly discuss whether you prefer writing in the personal or narrative styles that have been examined in this unit.

Moving On

The following pages provide six options for you to write about. Consider them carefully and choose one. You may choose to develop one of your earlier pieces from Steps 1 or 2.

1. Personal Writing

Write an extract from your autobiography. You should focus on one event or character only, as in 'A Painful Experience'. Some starting points might be:

a) a childhood memory

b) a first time experience

c) friends and enemies

d) good times, bad times

e) a major influence

f) I've never been so frightened

g) a painful experience.

Try to incorporate some of the techniques you have studied, including:

▶ an attention-grabbing opening

▶ a careful choice of vocabulary and sentence structure to achieve particular effects

▶ creating a sense of place

▶ revealing your thoughts and feelings about an event or episode.

There is further advice on planning this assignment in the next section (see page 165).

2. Narrative Writing

The first two options (a and b) are intended to be openings to stories. Your task is to complete them and give them a title.

If you choose to use one of these 'starters' for your original writing assignment, you could:

▶ change the voice to the third person if you find it easier to write as an observer

▶ add to or change any of the details given to make the writing more individual to you

▶ introduce other characters as your plot requires.

Think about the mood you are trying to create in your writing, whether it be mysterious, tense, threatening or humorous.

Now read each of the following options and decide which you will choose to complete. Plan possible ways of developing the story before beginning to write.

a Short Story – Untitled

> The rain eased to a steady drizzle as the train ground to a halt at platform 6, but the grey sky reflected my mood. Ten years earlier I had left from the same platform but now things were very different. Now, I was successful. Now, I had nothing to prove. Except to my parents. That is why I was back. I knew it wouldn't be easy – it would be a lot to ask – but I had to know if they had forgiven me.

b Short Story – Untitled

I'll never forget that day. It began just like many others, with the alarm bringing me out of sleep to the sounds of radio station Key 103. I remember thinking, not for the first time, I really must find something gentler for first thing in the morning. I still haven't done anything about that. I took my usual long shower, grabbed a quick coffee – strong, black, no sugar – and shuffled through the post. There wasn't anything that couldn't wait. I binned the junk mail unopened. I grabbed my laptop, set the alarm as I left the house, climbed into my car and eased it off the drive. So far, everything was as it should be. There was nothing to prepare me for what was to come.

c Use the pictures below in any way you wish to create a story. You might combine ideas from more than one picture if you wish.

d Use this extract as a stimulus, not an opening, for a piece of writing in which you either: write about the events which caused the man to become homeless, or write about a day in the man's life.

You step off the train and make your way to the exit. It is freezing and you turn up your collar to counter the cold. As you reach the station concourse, you are stopped by a young man who asks for money for a meal. He is young and shivering. You take pity on him and hand him a two-pound coin. You are a little embarrassed at how little difference it will make and manage to mumble that it must be hard on the streets on such a cold day. He nods and thanks you. You leave the station and catch a bus home. As you sit on the top deck, your mind turns to the young man and you wonder what has driven him to live like that and how he gets through each day.

Development

This flow chart should ensure that you:

- plan carefully to develop an interesting piece of work

- structure your work to achieve the best effect

- revise your work until it reads more fluently

- avoid silly mistakes.

◀Assignment 1: Personal Writing▶

Select an incident to write about.

Brainstorm all the events connected with it.

Arrange these into a chronological order and add your feelings at each stage.

Briefly note why it was so memorable or significant. For example, did you learn something about yourself or others? Did it change you or give you a new outlook on things? How do you think the other people involved would look back on the event?

Where can you add humour or detail to bring the scene and characters to life?

Write an attention-grabbing opening paragraph. This might be a surprising statement, a piece of dialogue or a reflection on the incident from after the event.

Continue the writing, remembering to experiment with a) using language to create effects and suggest your feelings, and b) shifts of time to avoid a dull sequence of events.

When you have finished, read it back to yourself. Have you included enough detail? Could a reader easily imagine the event and its significance to you? Add detail where necessary and improve accuracy.

Write a neat final draft.

Assignment 2: Narrative Writing Flow Chart

Select the short story that you are going to write.

Work out the plot. Remember that most stories follow the pattern of: Introduction, developing plot, complication or 'problem', crisis, and resolution. What is your story going to build up to? How will it be settled?

Plan your characters. Only have a few who you then describe and explore in detail. What are their backgrounds? Get inside their heads to explore their thoughts and feelings in the story. Dialogue should reflect the mood and personality of your characters. Don't use too much.

Decide on the setting. Again, describe this in detail using imagery and colour to 'paint' the scene for the reader. Keep your story within a short time frame.

Are you going to use a first or a third person narrator?

Write an attention-grabbing opening paragraph. This might be a surprising statement, a piece of dialogue or a reflection on the incident from after the event.

Continue the writing, remembering to experiment with a) using language and sentence structures to create effects , and b) shifts of time to avoid a dull sequence of events.

When you have finished, read it back to yourself. Have you included enough detail? Could a reader easily picture the scene and imagine the characters? Add detail where necessary and improve accuracy.

Write a neat final draft.

Review

Now it is time to plan your assignment. Use this opportunity to raise any concerns you may have over the task you have chosen or the writing process outlined above.

Step 5 – Boost Your Grade

Starting Point

Before writing your assignment, this Step will help you to:

▶ become familiar with the awarding body criteria for original writing

▶ check some of the writing you have encountered in the unit against the criteria

▶ compare your own writing skills to the Board criteria, and set your own targets.

The following table shows the examination criteria used to assess original writing. Examiners will read your assignment and decide how many of these skills you have achieved. Your mark will be based on their decision. For example, if you have achieved most of the skills used to describe a 'C' student, you will be awarded a mark which indicates a 'high C'. The more skills you can master, the higher the mark.

English Criteria Checklist		
Baseline Skills	**Additional Skills**	
Grade E	**Grade C**	**Grade A**
▶ develop planned accounts, including detailed ideas and descriptions ▶ match the style and form of writing to its purpose and to the reader ▶ begin to use sentence structures and vocabulary to achieve particular effects ▶ spell some irregular words accurately ▶ use punctuation to help clarify meaning	▶ vary writing styles, paragraphs and sentence structures to interest the reader ▶ create well structured accounts with well developed characters and settings and descriptions ▶ organise and punctuate your writing to help make meaning clear and coherent ▶ paragraphs should be used correctly to structure and make the meaning clear, spelling should be accurate	▶ write fluent, controlled and well-structured accounts ▶ give powerful accounts of real or imagined experiences ▶ use a range of sentence structures (both simple and complex) with accurate punctuation to produce intended effects ▶ paragraphs should be used to link and clarify the writing ▶ use mature and appropriate vocabulary with accurate spelling ▶ present work effectively in appropriate form(s)

Moving On

Depending on which type of assignment you have chosen, you will now look at a section from either 'A Painful Experience' or 'Dinner at Eight'. With your group, find examples of how the criteria for A and B have been satisfied. Be prepared to share your findings with the rest of the class.

Development

Use the table of criteria to make a realistic assessment of your own skills and identify your strengths and weaknesses.

It might help to use headings to set out your thoughts. You could use: 'Skills I have mastered' and 'Skills I need to work on'. If you do this carefully, you will have provided yourself with a set of targets for this unit.

The second of these lists will indicate the areas on which you will need to concentrate if you are to improve your grade.

Review

What have you learned about the skills and technical devices which combine to make a successful piece of original writing?

Media – Advertising

Introduction

Objectives

In successfully completing this unit, you will:

▶ study a selection of advertisements

▶ develop an understanding of media terms

▶ identify the key features of advertisements (text and moving images)

▶ develop ways of responding to media tasks

▶ plan a response to a media assignment

▶ draft, revise and proofread your response

▶ present your final piece of work for GCSE assessment.

GCSE

You will:

▶ complete a GCSE English coursework assignment for writing (EN3)

▶ develop the reading skills you need for the GCSE examination

▶ develop the writing skills you need for GCSE English

▶ complete a GCSE speaking and listening component in both group discussion and formal presentation.

Coursework and Examination Skills

▶ *Reading* – analytical reading of literary texts to demonstrate understanding

▶ *Writing* – writing to analyse, review and comment

▶ *Speaking and Listening* – working co-operatively with others in a group discussion.

Step 1 – *The Importance of Audience in Advertising*

In this unit, you are going to study the ways in which advertisers sell their products to consumers, and how advertisements are constructed. In this first Step, you will observe how the first consideration of any advertising agency is to think about who the product is aimed at. Agencies call the group of consumers who might buy the product its **target market** or **audience**.

Starting Point

1 Look at the following list of products and decide on the kinds of people you think are most likely to buy them. Write down the reasons for your choices.

a) baked beans

b) small hatchback car

c) double glazing

d) jeans

e) new range of sofas

f) trainers

g) computer games

h) new sports car

2 Now look at the following groups of people, or target audiences, and list at least five types of product you think they are likely to buy. Write down the reasons for your opinions.

a) people over 60 years old

b) young couples with no children

c) boys aged 5–11

d) girls aged 5–11

e) men aged 18–25

f) fathers and mothers with growing families

g) teenage girls aged 13–18

h) teenage boys aged 13–18

i) women aged 18–25

Key Concept

The group of people likely to buy a product differs according to each product. Only a section (or segment) of the buying public is likely to buy any one product – indeed, there are very few, if any, products that appeal to every buyer.

Advertisers have been quick to recognise this. Many satellite and cable television stations are aimed at minority groups, or **niche markets**, that will attract viewers with very specific interests. For example, a station may show only history programmes, cartoons or sports. As a result, those who advertise on these channels can be confident that their adverts are being watched by those people who are most likely to buy their products. This is known as **audience segmentation**.

Moving On

Share your thoughts with the rest of the class and discuss any differences in the opinions offered by other pairs.

Development

First, read the You Need to Know box opposite. Choose one of the target groups from Task 2 on page 170 and use the following prompts to help you build your own profile of a typical member of that group. Remember to keep a record of your ideas and to note reasons to support what you say. Consider your target group's:

▶ fashion or style tastes

▶ type of home and furnishings

▶ musical tastes

▶ leisure pursuits

▶ typical job (if applicable)

▶ holiday preferences

▶ favourite television programmes

▶ favourite foods

▶ ideal type of car (if applicable)

▶ ambitions.

Describe and discuss your profile with the rest of the class.

Review

What have you learned about

▷ the audiences for advertisements?

▷ audience segmentation?

▷ audience profiling?

Assignment Watch

In this Step, you have explored the way in which advertisers target their advertisements to attract their particular audiences. When analysing an advert, it is important to consider *who* it is aimed at.

Step 2 – The Psychology of Advertising

Advertising agencies are paid to ensure that advertisements attract their target audience. In the previous Step, you learned that these agencies spend a great deal of time researching what people in particular target groups say they want out of life. Their findings reveal much about the target group and help the advertising agency to form a clear view of that group's ambitions, the amount of disposable income, or spare money, they have to spend, and the kind of lifestyle they want.

Armed with this information, agencies try to produce advertisements that suggest that the product will provide some of the things the target group wants.

Starting Point

Advertising agencies begin by assuming that most people have the same basic needs and desires. They construct their advertisements by referring closely to these core instincts. This list shows some of the things that advertisers often think we all want from life.

▶ To be superior to others or part of a superior group.

▶ To keep up with others (such as neighbours or friends).

▶ To be up-to-date or a trendsetter.

▶ To be a member of a happy family.

▶ To be good-looking or beautiful.

▶ To be popular.

▶ To be wealthy.

Key Concept

A person's hopes and desires, such as those just listed, are known as their **aspirations**. These aspirations are the goals an individual hopes to achieve in life.

You are now going to look at an advertisement to decide on the target group for the product and the kind of lifestyle it suggests to the consumer.

Look at the advertisement for a Hugo Boss perfume on the following page and answer the following questions.

1 What does the way the girl is dressed and how she is looking at the camera suggest about her and the kind of life she leads?

2 What do the words 'expect everything' tell us about her aspirations?

3 Which of the qualities listed in the left hand column does the advertisement associate with a Hugo Boss woman?

4 What kind of woman do you think *Boss Woman* is aimed at? Think about her age group, job, hobbies and interests.

Share your answers with the rest of the class.

Moving On

You are now going to consider the selling techniques that advertisers use to promote a product to ensure that the product appeals to our aspirations. For example, if a person would like to be seen as a trendsetter, advertisements that suggest that a product is modern or new are more likely to appeal to him or her. Here are some of the selling techniques that advertising agencies use to attract buyers. The advertisers:

▶ claim that the product is new, modern or the 'latest'

▶ claim that the products is traditional and dependable, and that it represents 'quality'

▶ promote the feeling that the buyer is special or superior

▶ use humour or wit

▶ imply scientific or technological advances

▶ suggest that the product is the biggest or best

▶ use gimmicks

▶ suggest it is a bargain

▶ picture babies or children

▶ picture 'cute' animals

▶ suggest that the product is unusual or out of the ordinary.

1 For each selling technique on the list, name one advertisement (from a newspaper, magazine, the television or cinema) that uses that approach to promote its product.

2 Discuss the effect that each advertisement is likely to have on the consumer. Keep a record of your thoughts.

Development

You are now going to prepare a two minute presentation to give to the class based on one of the adverts you have listed in the last exercise.

1 Use the following prompts to prepare your presentation:

▶ the name of the product

▶ its target audience

▶ a summary or description of the advertisement

▶ the aspirations that the product suggests it will satisfy

▶ the technique(s) it uses to appeal to the viewer or reader.

2 Decide who is going to present your work to the class and practise your presentation.

Share your thoughts with the rest of the class.

Step 3 – The Language of Colour

Nothing ever appears in advertisements by accident, and this includes the use of colour. Advertisers recognise that colour is an important way of creating or reinforcing an impression. Research has shown that particular colours are associated with certain moods and feelings. In this Step you will examine the ways in which colour can be used to arouse reactions in a target audience.

Starting Point

1 Look again at the advertisement for the perfume *Boss Woman* on page 173. What do you make of the use of colour in the advert? What are the associations of black and white? How effective is it to set the woman against a black background?

2 Now look at the spidergram for the colour 'green'. Two words that you might associate with green have been provided. Note that they are used to imply very different things. Can you suggest some additional words?

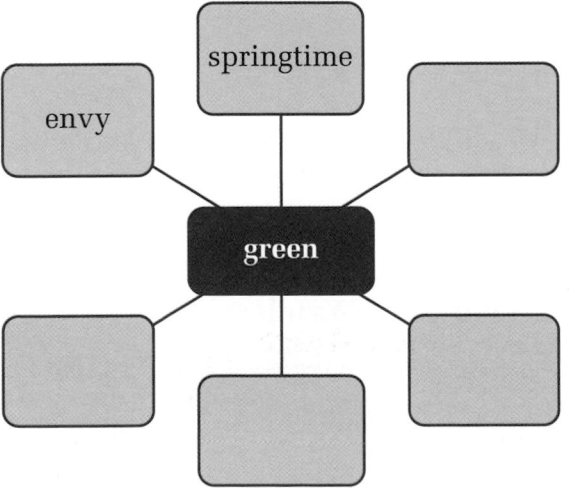

Moving On

For all of the colours in the following list, note at least two things you would associate with each one.

- ❯ black
- ❯ gold
- ❯ pink
- ❯ yellow
- ❯ grey
- ❯ red

Share your responses with the rest of the class, and discuss and explain any different interpretations that may arise.

Development

Key Concept

When a sign or symbol carries a meaning or suggestion additional to its everyday meaning, the secondary meaning is known as its **connotation**. For example, the colour white may be used in an advertisement to suggest purity or innocence, since it is a colour often associated with both qualities. However, it may also suggest a sense of emptiness or cold, and could be used as a background to imply that a setting is unwelcome or desolate.

It is the intention behind its use that will determine what the colour is meant to imply.

A colour can provoke positive or negative reactions, depending on the context in which it is used. You are now going to think about the use of colour in two specific advertisements.

If the colours in an advertisement are unsuitable, it may not work.

1 Look at the two advertisements printed on the pages 177 and 178. What are the main colours used in each one? What do you associate with these colours?

2 Discuss what kind of mood or association the advertiser is trying to create by the use of the chosen colour(s).

3 How do the colours reinforce the meaning of the words used in the advertisement? Discuss the reasons for your opinions and make a note of your thoughts.

Share your thoughts with the rest of the class.

Review

What have you learned about:

▸ the 'language of colour'?

▸ the importance of colour in advertising and the context in which colours are used?

Assignment Watch

In this Step you have seen how the use of colour plays an important part in the overall impact of an advertisement.

Stir up some passion **Sharwood's**

You Need to Know

It is often said that a single picture is worth a thousand words when it comes to describing a scene or event, or when creating an atmosphere. Advertising agencies, therefore, spend a great deal of time creating images that they hope will influence the way in which an audience reacts to a product.

As with colours, images have both a **denotation** and a **connotation**. The denotation is the common-sense, everyday meaning of something. For example, an engagement ring is a circular piece of precious metal, usually decorated with diamonds and sapphires. This is its denotation.

The connotation is the additional meaning something carries with it. For example, when a man gives a woman an engagement ring, he is offering her more than a simple piece of jewellery – an engagement ring means that she is to be married. That is its connotation.

In this Step, you are going to look at how advertisers use visual images to promote appropriate messages about the product for the target audience.

Starting Point

1 Look again at the advertisement for 100% Pure New Zealand on page 177. List the things that you can see in the photograph. (Ignore the words for this task.)

2 What is the overall impression of life in New Zealand that these elements combine to create? Make a note of your thoughts.

3 What are the denotations and connotations of the advert? Note down your ideas.

4 Now look at the images below. What are the denotations and connotations of each image?

5 Name five products you could advertise using each of these images and explain why the image has the correct connotations for the product. E.g. an astronaut might be an appropriate image to advertise a product that is considered 'state of the art', innovative technology.

Share your thoughts with the rest of the class.

Moving On

Now that you have thought about the way that images are constructed and the messages they carry, you are going to apply what you have learned in a practical exercise.

Imagine that the Tourist Information Board in your region has decided to produce a series of posters to promote your (nearest) town and the local area. You are a member of the advertising agency hired to make the advertisements and you have to decide on the images that you would use to attract visitors to the area. You will need to think about the kinds of people likely to visit the area, the beauty spots, any places of interest, the leisure facilities and any interesting local history.

1 Use the following prompts to help you jot down ideas on the image(s) you would use to advertise the town and the area as a holiday destination. Include:

▶ your target audience

▶ the kinds of interests the area has to offer a visitor

▶ any important buildings, like museums, theatres, sports grounds or swimming pools

▶ local landscapes or beauty spots

▶ cultural events such as plays, concerts, sporting competitions or fairs

▶ local history such as heritage centres, houses of important people, castles and battlefields

▶ important people who live, or have lived, in the area.

2 Make notes about what each choice would suggest about the area and the overall impression that your final selection of images would promote.

Development

Using the notes you have made, prepare a two to three minute presentation in which you explain to the Tourist Board the images you have decided to use and what they are intended to suggest about the area. Make sure that you include:

▶ the target audience you would aim to attract

▶ the overall impression you are trying to create

▶ the contribution that each of your chosen images makes to that impression

▶ how your use of colour might reinforce the image and influence audience response.

Make your presentation to the class.

Assignment Watch

In this Step you have looked at how audience reaction can be influenced by the careful selection of powerful visual images.

Step 5 – Working with Words 1 – Slogans

In addition to the visual images used in advertisements, the words used also play a vital part in creating and/or supporting an overall impression for the target audience.

The words may be used:

▶ as an extended description/explanation of the product

▶ in one or two sentences which capture what the product is meant to represent or provide – that is, how it fulfils the purchaser's needs and aspirations

▶ as a key phrase or sentence about the product.

Starting Point

Make a note of five examples of slogans from advertisements you know well.

Share your examples with the rest of the class.

Key Concept

A phrase or sentence used to summarise an important feature of a product is known as a slogan. A **slogan** is a way of establishing or 'anchoring' the meaning of the image in the advertisement, or of creating an impression about the product. For example, the words '100% Pure New Zealand' ensure that the reader realises that the image is of New Zealand and that it is unspoilt and natural.

Here are a three examples of slogans taken from advertisements:

▶ Making life taste better (Sainsbury's)

▶ Just do it (Nike)

▶ The future's bright, the future's orange (Orange mobile phones)

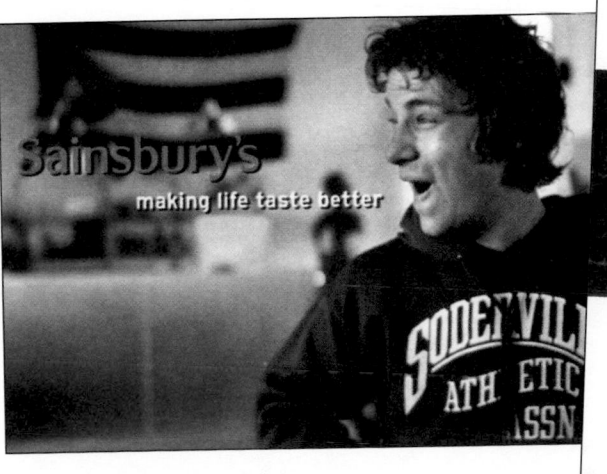

Moving On

In order to create 'catchy' slogans, advertisers often use one or more of the following techniques:

▶ word play – this includes the use of double meanings, songs or jingles, quotes, jokes, puns and commonly-used expressions

▶ repetition – this includes the use of rhyme, rhythm, alliteration and assonance

▶ deliberately breaking the rules – this includes misspelling words, making grammatical errors and leaving sentences unfinished.

For the following slogans and another two of your own choice:

1 Explain what the words suggest to the reader (the connotation).

2 Identify and explain the technique(s) being used.

▶ The car in front is a Toyota

▶ The cream of Manchester (Boddington's beer)

▶ Because you're worth it (L'Oreal cosmetic products)

▶ Once you pop, you just can't stop (Pringles crisps)

▶ p-p-pick up a Penguin! (chocolate biscuit)

Share your thoughts with the rest of the class.

Development

You are now going to apply the techniques you have learned to create some slogans of your own.

1 Choose three things that are currently being advertised on television or in print, for example:

▶ a supermarket

▶ a car

▶ mobile phones

▶ cosmetics

▶ a chocolate bar

▶ sportswear

▶ an item of clothing.

2 For each of your chosen products, use a different technique (i.e. wordplay, repetition or deliberately breaking the rules) to create a slogan.

Share your slogans with the rest of the class and talk about the technique you have used in each case. Then explain the effect you are trying to achieve.

Review

Discuss what have you learned about the types of writing you might find in an advertisement and the techniques advertisers might use to create slogans.

Step 6 – Working with Words 2 – Word Associations

In this Step, you are going to examine the way in which advertisers use specific words to influence the way that consumers feel or think about a product. By carefully selecting the words they use, advertisers hope to reinforce the image they are creating for the product.

If the advertiser wants to create the idea that the product is a luxury item, the copywriter will select words the reader may associate with wealth and comfort – and so the advert may include words such as 'pamper', 'spoil yourself', 'relax', 'elegant' or 'special'. For example, the campaign for the Boss perfume advert carried the following copy:

> Inspired by modern, strong and confident women, *Boss Woman* has style, is sophisticated and shows a perfect harmony between minimalism and femininity.

These words have strong associations (e.g. 'confident' = self-assured, 'harmony' = friendship and order) that create a picture of elegance, style and independence which the advertisers trust will appeal to its target audience.

Key Concept

When individual words suggest related ideas, this is known as **word association**.

Starting Point

For each of the words listed below, give five other words that could be associated with it. (It may help if you think in terms of selling a specific product.)

- successful
- attractive
- popular
- superior

Share your ideas with the rest of the class.

Moving On

Look at the advertisement for holidays in the Dominican Republic on page 184 and note any individual words that are used to create an impression of freedom and discovery.

Share your thoughts with the rest of the class.

Here, I feel free

Here, there's much more

than the Caribbean sun.

Much more than a thousand golden beaches,

much more than the rhythm of merengue.

Here, you will get the feel of life and peace,

feel the movement of history,

the joy of our people,

and the sounds of nature.

Here, an entire country awaits you.

A land of sensations.

The **DominicanRepublic**

a land of sensations

For more information check your travel agency or
the Tourism office of The Dominican Republic
Tel.: 020 7242 7778

GRUPO TENDER 2002

Development

In the advertisement for the Dominican Republic you will probably have noticed that the idea of discovering new sensations is reinforced throughout by the many words associated with that feeling. Now you are going to apply what you have learned to an advertisement for a completely different product.

1 Look at the advertisement for the Boots Botanics range of cosmetics on page 186. What is the overall impression that this advertisement suggests? Which words help to create this impression?

2 Use a dictionary and/or thesaurus to look up the words you have identified. Note how they trigger further word associations that support the overall impression suggested by the advertisement.

3 How do the visual images and the use of colour support the impression suggested by the words?

Share your responses with the rest of the class.

Review

Discuss what have you learned about word association and how impressions are created by words.

Assignment Watch

In the last two Steps you have learned how language is used to support visual images in creating impressions or feelings about a product.

BOTANICS uses modern science to harness the pure power of plants.

And the new Botanics cosmetics range is no exception.

For example, the Eye Colour in the Personal Eyes™ Magnetic Compact contains apple to protect and coconut to moisturise.

Whereas the Soothing and Calming Eye Base contains liquorice and horse chestnut to soothe skin and reduce puffiness.

So, whilst we're taking care of your make up, nature's taking care of your skin.

www.wellbeing.com

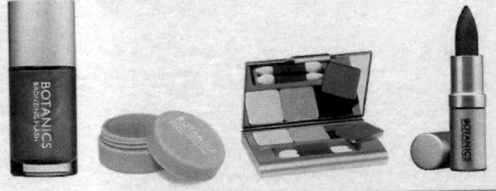

BOTANICS COSMETICS. ONLY AT BOOTS.

Ideas for life

Step 7 – The Moving Image 1

In this Step you are going to look at advertising on television and at the cinema where advertisers have the opportunity to use moving pictures as well as still images.

First, you need to know about the types of shots used by directors of advertisements. These will help you to analyse what you are watching and to describe the effects that advertisements are trying to achieve.

You Need to Know

Advertisers are extremely resourceful when it comes to finding ways of reaching potential customers. Steps 1 to 6 concentrated primarily on printed advertisements found in magazines and newspapers, or on advertising boards. Although advertising is to be found in a surprisingly diverse number of places – radio, direct mail, telemarketing, online advertising, catalogues, sponsorship, and even product placement in films – television is the most expensive and high-profile form. The advantages of television advertising are that:

▸ it is guaranteed to reach a specific audience (advertisers will be aware of viewing figures for a programme and will pay accordingly) and can be targeted at specific groups of consumers, according to when it's scheduled

▸ it is probable that potential customers will see the advert more than once (unless they actively change channel) and spend around 30 seconds or so viewing the advert each time – more time than they would spend looking at an advert in a magazine

▸ it allows advertisers to give more 'depth' to adverts – using narratives (storylines), music, voiceovers, etc. In effect, they have all the resources of a filmmaker at their disposal.

Starting Point

Listed below are the main types of camera shots used by film-makers.

Try to match the shots to the descriptions given below.

a long shot	**c** point-of-view shot
b medium shot	**f** panning-shot
c close-up	**g** high-angle shot
d extreme close-up	**h** low-angle shot

1 Shows the top half of someone's body and the setting in the background.

2 The viewer looks down on the subject. The character looks vulnerable and small.

3 The face of the character fills the frame. This is an excellent way of showing emotions.

4 The viewer sees what the character sees.

5 The viewer looks up at the subject. The character dominates the shot and looks powerful or confident.

6 Shows where a character is or where the action is taking place. The audience can see the 'big picture'.

7 The person fills most of the frame. The shot concentrates on head and shoulders. The audience is able to see the character's emotions.

8 The camera moves horizontally, following the action or shifting from one image to another.

Moving On

Here are examples of each of the shots mentioned above. Identify the shot used in each of the following images.

1 low-angle shot	5 panning-shot
2 extreme close-up	6 medium shot
3 high-angle shot	7 point-of-view shot
4 close-up	8 long shot

1 Share your responses with the rest of the class.

2 Look at the following stills taken from television advertisements and analyse the images used. Comment on:

▶ the type of shot

▶ the angle

▶ the setting

▶ the effect the shot is intended to have on the audience.

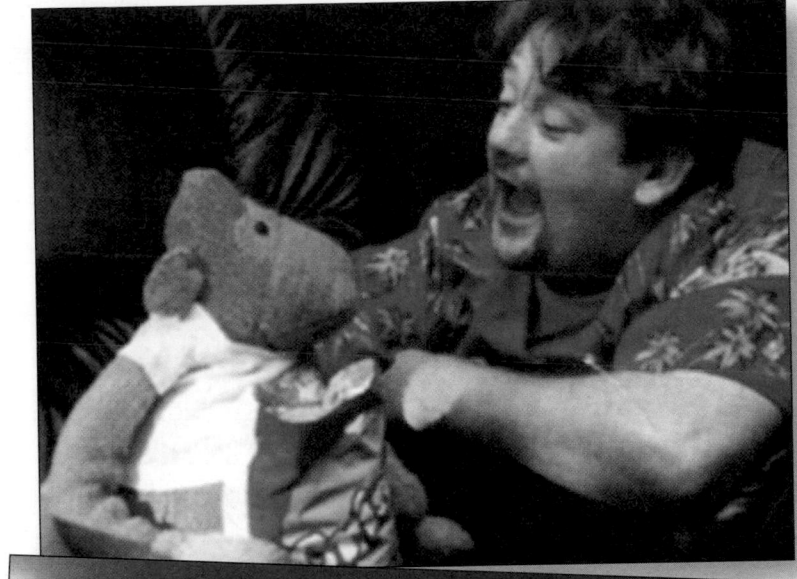

Development

Advertisements usually start with a storyboard.

Key Concept

A storyboard is a mock up of how a film sequence will, eventually, appear on screen. It consists of:

▶ instructions for the camera operator which tell him or her how long a shot will last and what type of shot it will be

▶ the way one shot will lead into another, e.g. using fade, dissolve or blackout

▶ the visual image that the camera will show

▶ the dialogue that will be heard at each stage

▶ the music or special effects that will be used

▶ an explanation of how the content and sequence of shots is selected through editing.

A basic storyboard is set out as follows. More information can be added if necessary – for example, the duration of each shot.

Woman: You can't have those, they're Sarah's.
Music: a saxophone playing in the background.

Man: OK.

Voice-over (celebrity): irresistible chocolate digestives.

Man stares at photo of Sarah.

Man eats biscuit. **Voice-over:** hmmm!

Man: (feigning tearful voice) Please don't eat my precious chocolate digestives!

Man gloats and laughs.

Man is caught by woman and flatmate (who look less than pleased). **Voice-over:** Make yourself at home.

You should now study at least one advertisement. You should watch it several times until you are familiar with the way it works. (Your teacher may provide an example for you.)

Produce a storyboard for the advertisement you have watched. Your response will not be judged on the quality of the artwork but on your ability to identify the component parts of the advertisement. Don't forget to show or identify the use of colour in your storyboard. Use the checklist in the Key Concept box on page 189 to ensure that you have included all the necessary detail.

Share your work with the rest of the class.

You Need to Know

When considering how much thought goes into the making of television adverts, it is worth bearing in mind that they can cost as much to make per second as big budget Hollywood films. To run an advert during a prime time hit show (and therefore reach a wide audience) will also be very expensive and so it is unsurprising that advertisers sometimes use star names both behind and in front of the camera.

When celebrities endorse products on television, it is immediately obvious to the viewer. What they may not know is that many famous film directors started their careers making adverts – Alan Parker (Bugsy Malone), Hugh Hudson (Chariots of Fire), Ridley Scott (Gladiator) and Tony Scott (Top Gun) – to name but a few.

A more recent example of this would be British director Simon West (Tomb Raider) who came to the attention of Hollywood having made the high-profile talking frogs campaign for a beer chain. These were broadcast extensively during the American Superbowl – the most expensive time slot in world television.

It has also been known for this to work the other way round. For example Cameron Crowe (Jerry Maguire) and the Coen Brothers (O Brother Where Art Thou?) have made adverts for a well known high street clothes store long after they had become well known and critically acclaimed in the film industry.

Review

What have you learned about the types of shots used in filming advertisements, the effects each type of shot might have on the viewer and the construction of a storyboard?

Assignment Watch

In this Step you have learned the media language used to describe camera shots and looked at the way ideas for moving image advertisements are prepared as storyboards. You have also discussed the effects that particular types of shot may have on viewers.

Step 8 – The Moving Image 2

Starting Point

1 Note five current adverts on television that you find memorable.

2 Why do you find them memorable? (Think about the music, people/characters, and look and feel of the advert.)

3 How were they trying to appeal to you? (Look back at Step 2)

Moving On

Advertising campaigns produced for television will often have a distinct 'feel' – that is, they use recurring characters, voice-overs, celebrity endorsements, specific styles of animation, running jokes and so on. The speed of editing and use of music depend heavily on what is being advertised. An advert for a soft drink that is trying to persuade its young audience that the product is fashionable may use quick editing to suggest excitement and vigour, whilst this will probably not be the approach when something 'practical' or 'serious' is being offered, such as adverts for washing powder or for a bank.

1 Using the five adverts you have already identified, make notes on:

▶ the product being advertised

▶ their potential audience – their age, amount of disposable income, gender, etc.

▶ the speed of the editing – are there lots of different shots or a long, lingering slow pace?

▶ the types of shots used

▶ the use of music – how does this affect the atmosphere of the advert?

▶ any voice-overs – is it a recognisable voice?

▶ any documentary or movie feel they have

▶ whether there is a celebrity endorsement – why is this celebrity suitable?

▶ if there is dialogue – is it informative? Entertaining? Both? Are slogans used?

2 Discuss your findings with the class. (Obviously, not all of the above will necessarily be present in one advert.)

Development

1 Plan a television advertising campaign for either a new chocolate bar, a clothing chain or a soft drink. Choose one.

2 Produce a storyboard for at least one advertisement, giving details of all of the relevant considerations above. You must also be able to explain why your campaign will be suitable for the product. Who will buy it? What techniques will you use?

Review

What have you learned about the techniques directors use to appeal to their targeted audiences in television adverts?

Assignment Watch

Should you choose to analyse a series of television advertisements, it is vital that you are able to identify the key points in the campaign – in terms of the audience the advert is aimed at and the ways in which the advertisers have chosen to appeal to this group of people.

Step 9 – Tackling the Assignment

Starting Point

For your GCSE coursework folder, you will be asked to submit one of the following assignments.

ⓘ

Read the following and choose the assignment about which you feel most confident.

Assignment 1

1 Select one advertisement and analyse the techniques it uses to target its intended audience. (You may use either a moving image or a printed advertisement for this task.) You could use any of the advertisements studied in this unit or your own choices.

Assignment 2

2 Look at the advertisements for The Dominican Republic and New Zealand (printed on pages 177 and 178). Analyse the ways in which each product is advertised and explain any similarities and differences between them.

Assignment 3

3 Through close reference to at least three advertisements, analyse the techniques advertisers use to attract and persuade their target audience(s).

(You may use either moving image and/or printed advertisements for this assignment.)

Moving On

Use the following chart to help you to plan your assignment.

Planning the assignment:		
Assignment	**Thinking:**	**Structure:**
1	This assignment allows you to focus on one advertisement in particular. For this question you should: ▸ consider its intended target audience ▸ think about the overall impression it suggests to its audience ▸ look at the use of colour ▸ consider why the image(s) is/are presented in the way(s) they are ▸ look at the use of (language) words. ▸ look at the use of print styles and fonts – the style of font may be intended to suggest certain qualities about the product or company ▸ think about the use of voice-overs or soundtracks and editing if applicable ▸ look at how the techniques are used to target (its) the intended reader or viewer	In your response, make sure that you: ▸ explain the aims and purpose of your writing ▸ briefly describe the advertisement and what it shows ▸ identify the audience targeted by the advertisement ▸ analyse each of the techniques used, in turn, and explain how it is intended to appeal to its audience, referring in detail to examples from the advertisement. ▸ explain whether it is successful in what it sets out to do.

Planning the assignment:		
Assignment	**Thinking:**	**Structure:**
2	This assignment adds the dimension of comparison to the first task. For each advertisement, you should consider: ▶ the intended target audience ▶ the overall impression suggested to the audience ▶ the use of colour ▶ the use of visual image ▶ the use of words. ▶ the similarities and differences between the two advertisements.	Look again at any notes you made about these advertisements. In your response, make sure that you: ▶ explain the aims and purpose of your writing ▶ briefly describe the advertisements and what they show ▶ compare the audiences targeted by the advertisements ▶ compare the way each advertisement uses colour, visual images and words (language) ▶ comment on how effectively the techniques are used in each advertisement ▶ express and explain any personal preference you may have.
	Thinking:	**Structure:**
3	This assignment is more wide ranging. In addition to analysis and comparison, it invites you to explore the way that advertisers use a range of techniques to target and persuade consumers to buy their products. It requires you to select suitable examples from a variety of advertisements to support the points you wish to make. For this question you should: ▶ consider how advertisers use their assumptions about their chosen audience to help them create an appropriate impression ▶ think about how each of the following contributes to the overall impression of the advertisements: colour, visual images, what the images suggest about someone's lifestyle or aspirations, the use of words (language).	In your response, make sure that you: ▶ explain the aims and purpose of your writing ▶ explain how advertisers' assumptions about particular target groups lead them to use stereotypical profiles that help them produce advertisements that reflect the needs and desires of their intended audiences In analysing the techniques, consider: ▶ why the images are presented in the way(s) they are ▶ what the images suggest about lifestyle(s) or aspirations ▶ the use of colour ▶ the words used, including fonts ▶ the use of voice-overs or soundtracks and editing if applicable ▶ how the techniques target their intended readers or viewers. Comment on how effectively the techniques are used in each advertisement.

(N.B. In any activity that requires comparison, organising your ideas into a simple grid often helps to make the important features on which you need to comment clearer. You might set out your initial thoughts about assignments 2 and 3 in three columns, with the features listed in column 1 and how each advertisement makes use of them in columns 2 and 3.)

Boost Your Grade

Before you start to write your assignment, you are going to examine what makes a successful response.

Listed below are the criteria that the examiner will use to assess your work. Read them carefully and use them to help you to assess the students' work that follows.

Starting Point

Read the criteria for Media and make a note of any words or phrases you do not understand.

English Criteria Checklist		
Grade E	**Grade C**	**Grade A**
You should: ▶ use **presentational devices** and **styles** of writing **appropriate** to **task, purpose** and **material** ▶ begin to **develop ideas** and **viewpoints** in some **detail**.	You should: ▶ present and **explain opinions, viewpoints** and **attitudes coherently** and **logically** ▶ use an **impersonal** style where **appropriate**, but show **engagement** with the task.	You should: ▶ express ideas **coherently, logically** and **persuasively** ▶ weigh **judiciously** a **range** of **views** and **opinions**.

(N.B. This requires the writer to make judgements about advertisements and justify opinions about their effectiveness.)

Discuss the criteria with your teacher and clear up any uncertainties you may have.

Moving On

The following three extracts are taken from responses written by students who were set the following assignment:

'Analyse the ways in which 100% Pure New Zealand and The Dominican Republic advertisements are presented, and explain what the differences between the two tell you about their brand identity'

Read the first extract and the examiner's comments that follow.

The advertisement shows a man and woman running on a beach in New Zealand. Their clothes are left on the beach and they seem to be having a good time. It is evening time and the sky is a beautiful colour. The whole picture is made to look like a desert island and is pure as it says in the slogan, 100% Pure New Zealand. In The Dominican Republic advertisement, there is one main image on the left showing a deserted beach. There are three smaller images on the right showing people rafting, playing golf and a peaceful looking building. The advertisers want the audience to see that there is a lot to see and do in The Dominican Republic and that a holiday in this country will be both interesting and relaxing.

Assessor's Comments

This extract shows the student trying to match the content of the advertisements to their intended purposes. There is (some) minimal use of media terms and the writer is beginning **to express ideas and viewpoints**. However, much of the work is **purely descriptive**, simply describing the contents of the advertisements rather than analysing their layout and use of language and colour. Spelling, punctuation and grammar are sound.

Grade awarded: E

Find some examples in the text to support the views underlined in the examiner's assessment.

Share your thoughts with the rest of the class.

Development

Read the following two extracts, one of which received a grade A and the other a grade C, and then answer the questions that follow.

Excerpt 2

Both advertisements use colour effectively. The New Zealand advertisement shows the beach at dusk. The colours are not bright but gentle and make the place look warm and pleasant. The slogan '100% Pure New Zealand' suggests that the island is unspoilt and the image chosen looks natural and beautiful. This is the sort of place that might attract people who want to get away from it all and relax in peace and quiet.

The colour in The Dominican Republic advertisement is bright and sunny. It appears to be very hot and the settings are attractive to look at. The advertisement suggests that a holiday in The Dominican Republic is bound to be a sunny one and is aimed at people who enjoy a range of activities.

The Dominican Republic advertisement uses a variety of beautiful and quite exotic images to highlight the attractions of the country: the deserted, unspoilt beaches, white water rafting, a golf course by the sea and an elegant villa in the early evening. Taken together, they suggest that there are many and varied facets to a holiday in The Dominican Republic, whether cultural and historic, beautiful and scenic or relaxing and fun. The slogan suggests that there are many varied activities and that a vacation there would have whatever a person needed to make the holidaymaker happy. It offers something for everyone and, therefore, the audience appeal is wide-ranging but it, also, offers variety for those who want more from a holiday than snapshots of ruins or a tan.

By contrast, the single image of New Zealand suggests a natural, relaxing holiday on a classic desert-island-style beach. The couple have discarded their clothes and are running freely through the seawater along a deserted beach. Unlike The Dominican Republic advertisement, this does not seek to present a cultural or many-faceted vacation but a chance to get away from it all and rest in a beautiful, unspoilt place. The use of the word 'pure' in the slogan reflects the fact that New Zealand (is unspoilt) remains relatively undeveloped and natural ideal for those who want to escape the hustle and bustle of life in the 21st century and enjoy as sense of freedom and total relaxation.

1 Decide which of these extracts was awarded grade A and which a grade C.

2 Use the criteria for grades A and C to write assessor's comments for each extract.

3 Find evidence from each extract to support the comments you have made

Share your thoughts with the rest of the class.

Review

1 What have you learned about the aspects in advertisements on which you need to comment in order to achieve good grades?

2 What have you learned about the sorts of observations you need to make and the way in which the criteria are used to assess your work?

Published by HarperCollinsPublishers Limited
77–85 Fulham Palace Rd
Hammersmith
London
W6 8JB

www.CollinsEducation.com

On-line support for schools and colleges

ISBN 00071099636

British Library Cataloguing in Publication Data

A catalogue record for this publication is available from the British Library.

Internal Design by Ken Vail Graphic Design, Cambridge
Cover Design by Barking Dog Art
Commissioned by Isabelle Zahar
Project Managed by Charlie Evans
Edited by Charlie Evans and Nancy Terry
Permissions by Gavin Jones

The publishers would like to thank Charles Evans for his outstanding
editorial contribution to this Student Book.

The publishers wish to thank Elizabeth Worthen, English Teacher at
Holland Park School for her valuable comments on the material.

Acknowledgements

Photos and illustrations:
The Ronald Grant Archive: p6, 21, 58, 61, 66, 80, 81, 87, 89, 102, 120, 129
Photostage (Donald Cooper): p12, 13 (all), 14, 108, 110, 111, 134, 140
Robbie Jack Photography: p24, 25, 40, 113, 116 , 121, 125
Corbis: p52 (bottom), 164 (top and bottom left), 179 (both)
The Culture Archive: p52 (top), 59, 74, 94, 96, 99,
The Performing Arts Library: p5, 15 (both), 31 (both), 34, 40
The Advertising Archive: p 181, 189 (both)
The Bridgman Art Library: p23
Mary Evans Archive: 54, 62, 68, 71
Mander and Mitchenson: p5 (Macbeth poster)
Science Photo Library: p163
PA Photos: 164 (right)
Phil Cutts: p131

Artwork:
Asa Anderson: p150, 172, 176
Janek Matsiak: 188, 190

Text:
All extracts from *An Inspector Calls* are reproduced by permission of PFD on behalf of the
Estate of JB Priestley. All extracts from *Blood Brothers* by Willy Russell are reproduced
with permission of Methuen Publishing Limited. The extract from *Dickens: The Biography*
by Peter Ackroyd is reproduced with permission of Vintage, a division of Random House.